FAVORITE BRAND NAME
CASSEROLES & ONE-DISH MEALS

Publications International, Ltd.

Pictured on the front cover: Chicken Enchiladas *(page 120).*

ISBN: 0-7853-2400-3

Manufactured in U.S.A.

8 7 6 5 4 3 2 1

Microwave Cooking: Microwave ovens vary in wattage. Use the cooking times as guidelines and check for doneness before adding more time.

FAVORITE BRAND NAME
CASSEROLES & ONE-DISH MEALS

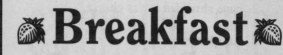 Breakfast

BONANZA

Ranch Quiche Lorraine

2 cups crushed butter-flavored crackers
6 tablespoons butter or margarine,
   melted
2 cups shredded Swiss cheese
4 eggs
2 cups heavy cream
1 package (1.2 ounces) HIDDEN
   VALLEY RANCH® Original Ranch®
   with Bacon salad dressing mix
1 tablespoon dehydrated minced onion

Preheat oven to 375°F. In medium bowl, combine crackers and butter. Press crumb mixture evenly into 10-inch pie pan or quiche dish. Bake until golden, about 7 minutes. Remove and cool pan on wire rack.

Increase oven temperature to 425°F. Sprinkle cheese over cooled pie crust. In medium bowl, whisk eggs until frothy. Add cream, salad dressing mix and onion. Pour egg mixture over cheese. Bake 15 minutes; reduce temperature to 350°F and continue baking until knife inserted in center comes out clean, about 20 minutes longer. Cool on wire rack 10 minutes before slicing. *Makes 8 servings*

Deep Dish Sausage Quiche

½ pound BOB EVANS FARMS® Original
    Recipe Roll Sausage
1 teaspoon butter or margarine
1 medium onion, chopped
1 unbaked prepared 9-inch deep dish pie
    crust
½ cup (2 ounces) shredded Swiss cheese,
    divided
4 eggs
1 cup milk
1 cup whipping cream
½ teaspoon salt
¼ teaspoon black pepper

Preheat oven to 425°F. Crumble sausage into medium skillet. Cook over medium heat until browned, stirring occasionally. Remove sausage to paper towels; set aside. Add butter and onion to drippings. Cook 5 minutes or until onion is tender. Cover bottom of pie crust with sausage, onion and ¼ cup cheese. Combine remaining ¼ cup cheese, eggs, milk, cream, salt and pepper in medium bowl; mix well and pour over sausage mixture. Bake 15 minutes. *Reduce oven temperature to 350°F.* Bake about 20 minutes more or until browned and well set. Let stand 5 minutes before cutting into wedges; serve hot. Refrigerate leftovers.

Makes 6 servings

Old Country Quiche

½ cup chopped onion
2 tablespoons butter
6 slices cooked bacon, crumbled
2 cups (8 ounces) shredded Wisconsin
   Swiss cheese
2 tablespoons all-purpose flour
3 eggs, beaten
1 cup milk
½ teaspoon salt
   Dash ground nutmeg
1 (9-inch) pastry shell, baked

Preheat oven to 400°F. Cook and stir onion in butter in small skillet until tender. Combine cooked onion, bacon, cheese and flour in small bowl. Combine eggs, milk, salt and nutmeg in large bowl. Stir in onion mixture. Pour into pastry shell. Bake 25 to 35 minutes or until center is set.   *Makes 6 servings*

Favorite recipe from **Wisconsin Milk Marketing Board**

Spinach Quiche

½ cup chopped onion
1 clove garlic, crushed
1 teaspoon margarine
1 (10-ounce) package frozen chopped
   spinach, thawed and well drained
1 (9-inch) pastry crust, unbaked
1 cup EGG BEATERS® Healthy Real Egg
   Product
1 cup skim milk
1 tablespoon all-purpose flour
1 teaspoon dried basil leaves
¾ teaspoon liquid hot pepper seasoning

In medium nonstick skillet, over medium-high heat, sauté onion and garlic in margarine until tender; add spinach. Spoon into bottom of pie crust; set aside.

In small bowl, combine Egg Beaters®, milk, flour, basil and liquid hot pepper seasoning; pour evenly over spinach mixture. Bake at 350°F for 45 to 50 minutes or until knife inserted into center comes out clean. Let stand 10 minutes before serving.

Makes 8 servings

Salmon Quiche: Prepare as above substituting 1 (7¾-ounce) can low-sodium salmon, drained and flaked, for spinach and 1 teaspoon dried dill weed for basil. Omit liquid hot pepper seasoning.

Double Onion Quiche

3 cups thinly sliced yellow onions
3 tablespoons butter or margarine
1 cup thinly sliced green onions
3 eggs
1 cup heavy cream
½ cup grated Parmesan cheese
¼ teaspoon hot pepper sauce
1 package (1 ounce) HIDDEN VALLEY®
    Milk Recipe Original Ranch® salad
    dressing mix
1 (9-inch) deep-dish pastry shell, baked
    and cooled

Preheat oven to 350°F. In medium skillet, sauté yellow onions in butter, stirring occasionally, about 10 minutes. Add green onions and cook 5 minutes longer. Remove from heat and let cool.

In large bowl, whisk eggs until frothy. Whisk in cream, cheese, pepper sauce and salad dressing mix. Stir in onion mixture. Pour egg-onion mixture into pastry shell. Bake until top is browned and knife inserted into center comes out clean, 35 to 40 minutes. Cool on wire rack 10 minutes before slicing. Garnish if desired.

Makes 8 servings

Broccoli & Cheese Quiche

2 cups zwieback crumbs
½ teaspoon ground nutmeg
⅛ cup honey
2 cups fresh broccoli florets or frozen
     broccoli florets, thawed and drained
½ tablespoon unsalted butter substitute
1 cup chopped yellow onion
1 cup (4 ounces) shredded ALPINE
     LACE® Reduced Fat Swiss Cheese
1 cup (4 ounces) shredded ALPINE
     LACE® Reduced Fat Colby Cheese
1 cup chopped red bell pepper
¾ cup egg substitute *or* 3 large eggs
2 large egg whites
¾ cup 2% lowfat milk
½ teaspoon dry mustard
½ teaspoon salt
¼ teaspoon freshly ground white pepper

1. Preheat the oven to 400°F. Spray a 10-inch pie plate with nonstick cooking spray. To make the crumb crust: Toss the crumbs and nutmeg with the honey until the crumbs are thoroughly coated. Press onto the bottom and up the side of the pie plate.

2. To make the filling: Coarsely chop the broccoli. Half-fill a medium-size saucepan with water and bring to a boil over medium-high heat. Add the broccoli and cook, uncovered, for 5 minutes or just until crisp-tender. Drain.

3. In a small nonstick skillet, melt the butter over medium-high heat. Add the onion and sauté for 5 minutes or until soft. Layer both of the cheeses, then the onion, bell pepper and broccoli in the crust.

4. In a medium-size bowl, whisk the egg substitute (or the whole eggs), the egg whites, milk, mustard, salt and pepper until blended. Pour over the vegetables.

5. Bake for 10 minutes. Reduce the oven temperature to 350°F. Bake 20 minutes longer or until golden brown and puffy and a knife inserted in the center comes out clean. *Makes 8 servings*

Quiche Lorraine Florentine

1 (10-ounce) package frozen chopped
   spinach, thawed and well drained
1 cup (4 ounces) shredded Swiss cheese
4 slices bacon, cooked and crumbled
2 tablespoons chopped green onions
1 (9-inch) unbaked pastry shell
3 eggs, slightly beaten
1 cup light cream or half-and-half
¼ cup GREY POUPON® Dijon Mustard

Combine spinach, cheese, bacon and green onions. Spoon mixture evenly into pastry shell.

In small bowl, blend eggs, cream and mustard. Pour evenly over spinach mixture. Bake at 375°F for 35 to 40 minutes or until knife inserted into center comes out clean. Let stand 10 minutes before serving.

Makes 8 servings

Sausage & Apple Quiche

1   unbaked (9-inch) pastry shell
½   pound bulk spicy pork sausage
½   cup chopped onion
¾   cup shredded, peeled tart apple
1   tablespoon lemon juice
1   tablespoon sugar
⅛   teaspoon red pepper flakes
1   cup (4 ounces) shredded Cheddar
      cheese
3   eggs
1½ cups half-and-half
¼   teaspoon salt
     Ground black pepper

1. Preheat oven to 425°F.

2. Place piece of foil inside pastry shell; partially fill with uncooked beans or rice. Bake 10 minutes. Remove foil and beans; continue baking pastry 5 minutes or until lightly browned. Let cool.

3. Reduce oven temperature to 375°F.

4. Crumble sausage into large skillet; add onion. Cook over medium heat until meat is browned and onion is tender. Spoon off and discard pan drippings.

5. Add apple, lemon juice, sugar and red pepper to skillet. Cook on medium-high, stirring constantly, 4 minutes or until apple is just tender and all liquid is evaporated. Let cool.

6. Spoon sausage mixture into pastry shell; top with cheese. Whisk eggs, half-and-half, salt and dash black pepper in medium bowl. Pour over sausage mixture.

7. Bake 35 to 45 minutes or until filling is puffed and knife inserted into center comes out clean. Let stand 10 minutes before serving.   *Makes 6 servings*

Salami Quiche

    4   eggs *or* 1 cup cholesterol-free egg
          substitute
    ⅔   cup parve nondairy creamer
    ½   teaspoon salt
    ¼   teaspoon freshly ground black pepper
    1½ cups (6 ounces) **HEBREW NATIONAL®**
          Beef Salami or Lean Beef Salami
          Chub, diced
    ½   cup sliced fresh mushrooms
    ½   cup quartered zucchini slices
    ¼   cup sliced green onions, including tops
    1   (9-inch) unbaked parve pie crust*

Preheat oven to 350°F. Beat eggs in large bowl. Add creamer, salt and pepper; beat well. Stir salami, mushrooms, zucchini and green onions into egg mixture; pour into pie crust. Bake 50 minutes or until golden brown and center is set. Let stand 5 minutes.

Makes 6 servings

*If parve pie crust is not available, prepare your favorite homemade pastry using parve margarine.

Turkey and Rice Quiche

   3 **cups cooked rice, cooled to room**
         temperature
  1½ **cups chopped cooked turkey**
   1 **medium tomato, seeded and finely diced**
   ½ **cup skim milk**
   3 **eggs, beaten**
   ¼ **cup sliced green onions**
   ¼ **cup finely diced green bell pepper**
   1 **tablespoon chopped fresh basil *or***
         1 teaspoon dried basil
   ½ **teaspoon seasoned salt**
   ⅛ **to ¼ teaspoon ground red pepper**
         Nonstick cooking spray
   ½ **cup (2 ounces) shredded Cheddar**
         cheese
   ½ **cup (2 ounces) shredded mozzarella**
         cheese

Combine rice, turkey, tomato, milk, eggs, onions, bell
pepper, basil, salt and red pepper in 13×9-inch pan
coated with cooking spray. Top with cheeses. Bake at
375°F for 20 minutes or until knife inserted near
center comes out clean. To serve, cut quiche into
8 squares; cut each square diagonally into 2 triangles.

Makes 8 servings

Favorite recipe from **USA Rice Council**

Easy Crab Asparagus Pie

- 4 ounces crabmeat, shredded
- 12 ounces fresh asparagus, cut into 1-inch pieces and cooked
- ½ cup chopped onion, cooked
- 1 cup (4 ounces) shredded Monterey Jack cheese
- ¼ cup grated Parmesan cheese
  Freshly ground pepper
- ¾ cup all-purpose flour
- ¾ teaspoon baking powder
- ½ teaspoon salt
- 2 tablespoons cold butter or margarine
- 1½ cups milk
- 4 eggs, slightly beaten

1. Preheat oven to 350°F. Lightly grease 10-inch quiche dish or pie plate.

2. Layer crabmeat, asparagus and onion in prepared pie plate; top with cheeses. Season with pepper.

3. Combine flour, baking powder and salt in large bowl. With pastry blender or 2 knives, cut in butter until mixture forms coarse crumbs. Stir in milk and eggs; pour over cheese mixture.

4. Bake 30 minutes or until filling is puffed and knife inserted near center comes out clean. Serve hot.

Makes 6 servings

Garden Omelet

3 teaspoons butter or margarine, divided
⅓ cup chopped onion
⅓ cup chopped red bell pepper
½ cup sliced mushrooms
½ teaspoon dried basil leaves
4 eggs, beaten
1 tablespoon milk
¼ teaspoon black pepper
Dash salt
½ cup (2 ounces) shredded Swiss cheese

1. Melt 1 teaspoon butter in large nonstick skillet over medium heat. Cook and stir onion and bell pepper 2 to 3 minutes or until onion is tender. Add mushrooms and basil; cook and stir 3 to 5 minutes more. Remove vegetables from skillet and keep warm.

2. Whisk together eggs, milk, black pepper and salt in medium bowl. Melt remaining 2 teaspoons butter in same skillet over medium heat; rotate pan to coat bottom. Pour egg mixture into skillet. Cook over medium heat; as eggs begin to set, gently lift edges of omelet with spatula and tilt skillet so that uncooked portion flows underneath.

3. When eggs are fully cooked, spoon vegetable mixture over half of omelet. Sprinkle with cheese. Loosen omelet with spatula and fold in half. Transfer to warm serving plate.   *Makes 2 servings*

Cheesy Salsa Omelet

1 cup egg substitute
1 tablespoon skim milk
   Nonstick cooking spray
¼ cup sliced fresh mushrooms
¼ cup chopped green onions
¼ cup GUILTLESS GOURMET® Nacho
      Dip (mild or spicy)
¼ cup GUILTLESS GOURMET® Salsa
      (mild, medium or hot)

Combine egg substitute and milk in small bowl; beat
well. Coat medium nonstick skillet with cooking spray;
heat over medium-high heat until hot. Add
mushrooms and onions; cook and stir 2 to 3 minutes
or until vegetables are softened. Remove vegetables
from skillet; set aside.

Add egg mixture to same skillet; cook over low heat
until egg mixture sets, gently lifting edge with spatula
to allow uncooked egg to flow under cooked portion.
Do not stir. Top with reserved vegetable mixture. Drop
spoonfuls nacho dip over vegetable mixture. Cover
tightly; let stand 3 to 5 minutes. Fold omelet in half.
Gently slide onto warm serving platter. Cut in half;
serve each half with 2 tablespoons salsa.

Makes 2 servings

Vegetable Omelet

Ratatouille (recipe follows)
5 whole eggs
6 egg whites *or* ¾ cup cholesterol-free egg
   substitute
¼ cup skim milk
½ teaspoon salt
⅛ teaspoon black pepper
4 to 6 slices Italian bread
2 cloves garlic, halved

1. Prepare Ratatouille. Keep warm.

2. Spray 12-inch skillet with nonstick cooking spray; heat over medium heat. Beat whole eggs, egg whites, milk, salt and pepper in large bowl until foamy. Pour egg mixture into skillet; cook over medium-high heat 2 to 3 minutes or until bottom of omelet is set. Reduce heat to medium-low. Cover; cook 8 minutes or until top of omelet is set. Remove from heat.

3. Spoon half the Ratatouille into center of omelet. Carefully fold omelet in half; slide onto serving plate. Spoon remaining Ratatouille over omelet.

4. Toast bread slices; rub both sides of warm toast with cut garlic cloves. Serve with omelet. Serve with fresh fruit, if desired.   *Makes 4 to 6 servings*

Ratatouille

1 cup chopped onion
½ cup chopped green bell pepper
2 cloves garlic, minced
4 cups cubed unpeeled eggplant
1 medium yellow summer squash, sliced
1 cup chopped fresh tomatoes
¼ cup finely chopped fresh basil *or*
    1½ teaspoons dried basil leaves
1 tablespoon finely chopped fresh
    oregano *or* 1 teaspoon dried oregano
    leaves
2 teaspoons finely chopped fresh thyme
    or ½ teaspoon dried thyme leaves

Spray large skillet with nonstick cooking spray; heat over medium heat. Add onion, bell pepper and garlic; cook and stir 5 minutes or until tender. Add eggplant, summer squash, tomatoes, basil, oregano and thyme. Cover; cook over medium heat 8 to 10 minutes or until vegetables are tender. Uncover; cook 2 to 3 minutes or until all liquid is absorbed.　　*Makes about 4 cups*

Western Omelet

½ **cup finely chopped red or green bell
pepper**
⅓ **cup cubed cooked potato**
2 **slices turkey bacon, diced**
¼ **teaspoon dried oregano leaves**
2 **teaspoons margarine, divided**
1 **cup EGG BEATERS® Healthy Real Egg
Product**
Fresh oregano sprig, for garnish

In 8-inch nonstick skillet, over medium heat, sauté bell
pepper, potato, turkey bacon and dried oregano in
1 teaspoon margarine until tender.* Remove from
skillet; keep warm.

In same skillet, over medium heat, melt remaining
margarine. Pour Egg Beaters® into skillet. Cook, lifting
edges to allow uncooked portion to flow underneath.
When almost set, spoon vegetable mixture over half of
omelet. Fold other half over vegetable mixture; slide
onto serving plate. Garnish with fresh oregano.

Makes 2 servings

*For frittata, sauté vegetables, turkey bacon and dried oregano in
2 teaspoons margarine. Pour Egg Beaters evenly into skillet over
vegetable mixture. Cook without stirring 4 to 5 minutes or until
cooked on bottom and almost set on top. Carefully turn frittata; cook
1 to 2 minutes more or until done. Slide onto serving platter; cut
into wedges to serve.

Mexican Frittata

2 whole eggs
4 egg whites
2 tablespoons skim milk
¼ teaspoon coarsely ground black pepper
  Nonstick cooking spray
¼ cup chopped red bell pepper
¼ cup chopped green onions
¼ cup sliced fresh mushrooms
¼ cup GUILTLESS GOURMET® Mild
  Nacho Dip
¼ cup GUILTLESS GOURMET® Roasted
  Red Pepper Salsa

Combine eggs, egg whites, milk and black pepper in small bowl; beat well. Coat medium nonstick skillet with cooking spray; heat skillet over medium-high heat until hot. Add red pepper, onions and mushrooms; cook and stir until tender. Remove vegetables from skillet; set aside.

Add egg mixture to same skillet; cook over low heat until egg mixture is set, gently lifting edge with spatula to allow uncooked egg to flow under cooked portion. *Do not stir.* Drop spoonfuls nacho dip on top. Top with vegetables. Cover; let stand 3 to 5 minutes. Cut in half; serve with salsa.   *Makes 2 servings*

Sausage Vegetable Frittata

5 eggs
¼ cup milk
2 tablespoons grated Parmesan cheese
½ teaspoon dried oregano leaves
½ teaspoon black pepper
1 (10-ounce) package BOB EVANS
    FARMS® Skinless Link Sausage
2 tablespoons butter or margarine
1 small zucchini, sliced (about 1 cup)
½ cup shredded carrot
⅓ cup sliced green onions with tops
¾ cup (3 ounces) shredded Swiss cheese

Whisk eggs in medium bowl; stir in milk, Parmesan
cheese, oregano and pepper. Set aside. Cook sausage in
large skillet over medium heat until browned, turning
occasionally. Drain off any drippings. Remove sausage
from skillet and cut into ½-inch lengths. Melt butter in
same skillet. Add zucchini, shredded carrot and onions;
cook and stir over medium heat until tender. Top with
sausage, then Swiss cheese. Pour egg mixture over
vegetable mixture. Stir gently to combine. Cook,
without stirring, over low heat, 8 to 10 minutes or
until center is almost set. Remove from heat. Let stand
5 minutes before cutting into wedges; serve hot.
Refrigerate leftovers.   *Makes 4 to 6 servings*

Hash Brown Frittata

1 (10-ounce) package BOB EVANS
   FARMS® Skinless Link Sausage
6 eggs
1 (12-ounce) package frozen hash brown
   potatoes, thawed
1 cup (4 ounces) shredded Cheddar
   cheese
⅓ cup whipping cream
¼ cup chopped green and/or red bell
   pepper
¼ teaspoon salt
   Dash black pepper

Preheat oven to 350°F. Cut sausage into bite-size pieces. Cook in small skillet over medium heat until lightly browned, stirring occasionally. Drain off any drippings. Whisk eggs in medium bowl; stir in sausage and remaining ingredients. Pour into greased 2-quart casserole dish. Bake, uncovered, 30 minutes or until eggs are almost set. Let stand 5 minutes before cutting into squares; serve hot. Refrigerate leftovers.

Makes 6 servings

Bacon & Potato Frittata

2 **cups frozen O'Brien-style potatoes with onions and peppers**
3 **tablespoons butter or margarine**
5 **eggs**
½ **cup canned real bacon pieces**
¼ **cup half-and-half or milk**
⅛ **teaspoon salt**
⅛ **teaspoon black pepper**

1. Preheat broiler. Place potatoes in a microwavable medium bowl; microwave on HIGH 1 minute.

2. Melt butter in large ovenproof skillet over medium-high heat. Swirl butter up side of pan. Add potatoes; cook 3 minutes, stirring occasionally.

3. Beat eggs in medium bowl. Add bacon, half-and-half, salt and black pepper; mix well.

4. Pour egg mixture into skillet; reduce heat to medium. Stir gently to incorporate potatoes. Cover and cook 6 minutes or until eggs are set at edges (top will still be wet).

5. Transfer skillet to broiler. Broil 4 inches from heat about 1 to 2 minutes or until center is set and frittata is golden brown. Cut into wedges.

Makes 4 servings

Spicy Crabmeat Frittata

1 tablespoon olive oil
1 medium green bell pepper, finely
    chopped
2 cloves garlic, minced
6 eggs
1 can (6½ ounces) lump white crabmeat,
    drained
¼ teaspoon ground black pepper
¼ teaspoon salt
¼ teaspoon hot pepper sauce
1 large ripe plum tomato, seeded and
    finely chopped

1. Preheat broiler. Heat oil in 10-inch broiler-proof nonstick skillet over medium-high heat. Add bell pepper and garlic; cook 3 minutes or until softened.

2. While bell pepper and garlic cook, beat eggs in medium bowl. Add crabmeat; mix to break large pieces. Add black pepper, salt and pepper sauce; blend well. Set aside.

3. Add tomato to skillet; cook and stir 1 minute. Add egg mixture to skillet. Reduce heat to medium-low; cook about 7 minutes or until eggs begin to set around edges.

4. Remove pan from burner and place under broiler 6 inches from heat. Broil about 2 minutes or until top of frittata is browned. Remove pan from broiler; slide frittata onto serving plate. Serve immediately.

Makes 4 servings

Garden Frittata

1   tablespoon extra-virgin olive oil
1   cup sliced, unpeeled, small red-skinned
    potatoes (about 4 ounces)
½   cup chopped red onion
½   cup chopped red bell pepper
1   teaspoon minced garlic
1   cup chopped fresh asparagus
½   cup fresh corn kernels or frozen corn,
    thawed and drained
1   cup diced ALPINE LACE® Boneless
    Cooked Ham (4 ounces)
¾   cup egg substitute *or* 3 large eggs
3   large egg whites
1   cup (4 ounces) shredded ALPINE
    LACE® Reduced Fat Lightly Smoked
    Provolone Cheese
¼   cup slivered fresh basil leaves *or*
    1 tablespoon dried basil
½   teaspoon salt
¼   teaspoon freshly ground black pepper

1. Preheat the broiler. In a large broiler-proof nonstick skillet, heat the oil over medium-high heat. Add the potatoes, onion, bell pepper and garlic. Cook, stirring occasionally, for 7 minutes or until the potatoes are almost tender. Stir in the asparagus, corn and ham and cook 3 minutes more or until the vegetables are crisp-tender.

2. In a medium-size bowl, whisk the egg substitute (or the whole eggs), the egg whites, cheese, basil, salt and black pepper together until blended. Pour over the vegetables. Reduce the heat and cook, uncovered, for 8 minutes or just until the egg mixture is set around the edges.

3. Slide the skillet under the broiler for 1 minute or until the eggs are set in the center. Serve immediately.

Makes 4 servings

Chicken Broccoli Frittata

1   cup chopped fresh broccoli flowerets
½   cup chopped cooked chicken
¼   cup chopped tomato
¼   cup chopped onion
¼   teaspoon dried tarragon leaves
1   tablespoon margarine
1   cup EGG BEATERS® Healthy Real Egg
      Product

In 10-inch nonstick skillet, over medium heat, sauté broccoli, chicken, tomato, onion and tarragon in margarine until tender-crisp. Reduce heat to low. Pour Egg Beaters® evenly into skillet over chicken mixture. Cover; cook 5 to 7 minutes or until cooked on bottom and almost set on top. Slide onto serving platter; cut into wedges to serve.

Makes 2 servings

Cheese Strata

BASIC STRATA
- 3 tablespoons butter or margarine
- 6 slices bread, crusts removed
- 3 cups (12 ounces) shredded Cheddar cheese
- 6 eggs
- 2 cups milk
- 1 tablespoon LAWRY'S® Minced Onion with Green Onion Flakes
- 1 teaspoon LAWRY'S® Seasoned Salt
- ¼ teaspoon LAWRY'S® Garlic Powder with Parsley

Lightly grease 13×9×2-inch baking dish with butter; arrange bread slices in bottom of dish. Sprinkle with half of Cheddar cheese. In medium bowl, beat together eggs, milk, Minced Onion with Green Onion Flakes, Seasoned Salt and Garlic Powder with Parsley. Pour mixture over bread and cheese. Sprinkle with remaining Cheddar cheese. Bake, uncovered, in 350°F oven 35 minutes or until light golden brown. Let stand 5 minutes before serving.   *Makes 6 servings*

Herb Strata: Add 2 tablespoons LAWRY'S® Pinch of Herbs to BASIC STRATA egg-and-milk mixture.

Italian-Herb Strata: To HERB variation, add ¼ cup sliced black olives to each cheese layer and top with diced tomatoes. Serve with LAWRY'S® Original-Style Spaghetti Sauce Spices & Seasonings prepared as directed on package.

Cheddar Cheese Strata

1   pound French bread, cut into ½- to
    ¾-inch slices, crusts removed, divided
2   cups (8 ounces) shredded reduced-fat
    Cheddar cheese, divided
2   whole eggs
3   egg whites
4   cups skim milk
1   teaspoon grated fresh onion
1   teaspoon dry mustard
½   teaspoon salt
    Paprika to taste

1. Spray 13×9-inch glass baking dish with nonstick cooking spray. Place half the bread slices in bottom of prepared dish, overlapping slightly if necessary. Sprinkle with 1¼ cups cheese. Place remaining bread slices on top of cheese.

2. Whisk whole eggs and egg whites in large bowl. Add milk, onion, mustard and salt; whisk until well blended. Pour evenly over bread and cheese. Cover with remaining ¾ cup cheese and sprinkle with paprika. Cover and refrigerate 1 hour or overnight.

3. Preheat oven to 350°F. Bake strata about 45 minutes or until cheese is melted and bread is golden brown. Let stand 5 minutes before serving.

Makes 8 servings

Cheddar and Leek Strata

8   eggs, lightly beaten
2   cups milk
½   cup beer
2   cloves garlic, minced
¼   teaspoon salt
¼   teaspoon black pepper
1   loaf (16 ounces) sourdough bread, cut
     into ½-inch cubes
2   small leeks, coarsely chopped
1   red bell pepper, chopped
1½ cups (6 ounces) shredded Swiss cheese
1½ cups (6 ounces) shredded sharp
     Cheddar cheese

1. Combine eggs, milk, beer, garlic, salt and black pepper in large bowl. Beat with wire whisk until well blended.

2. Place ½ of bread cubes on bottom of greased 13×9-inch baking dish. Sprinkle ½ of leeks and ½ of bell pepper over bread cubes. Top with ¾ cup Swiss cheese and ¾ cup Cheddar cheese. Repeat layers with remaining ingredients, ending with Cheddar cheese.

3. Pour egg mixture evenly over top. Cover tightly with plastic wrap or foil. Weight down top of strata with slightly smaller baking dish. Refrigerate strata at least 2 hours or overnight.

4. Preheat oven to 350°F. Bake strata uncovered 40 to 45 minutes or until center is set. Serve immediately.
Makes 12 servings

Spinach-Cheese Strata

- 6 slices whole wheat bread
- 2 tablespoons butter or margarine, softened
- 1 cup (4 ounces) shredded Cheddar cheese
- ½ cup (2 ounces) shredded Monterey Jack cheese
- 1¼ cups milk
- 6 eggs, lightly beaten
- 1 package (10 ounces) frozen spinach, thawed and well drained
- ¼ teaspoon salt
- ⅛ teaspoon pepper

1. Spread bread with butter; arrange buttered-side up in single layer in greased 13×9-inch baking dish. Sprinkle with cheeses.

2. Combine milk, eggs, spinach, salt and pepper in large bowl; stir well. Pour over bread and cheese. Cover; refrigerate at least 6 hours or overnight.

3. Bake, uncovered, at 350°F about 1 hour or until puffy and lightly golden.   *Makes 4 to 6 servings*

Easy Morning Strata

1 pound BOB EVANS FARMS® Original Recipe Roll Sausage
8 eggs
10 slices bread, cut into cubes (about 10 cups)
3 cups milk
2 cups (8 ounces) shredded Cheddar cheese
2 cups (8 ounces) sliced fresh mushrooms
1 (10-ounce) package frozen cut asparagus, thawed and drained
2 tablespoons butter or margarine, melted
2 tablespoons all-purpose flour
1 tablespoon dry mustard
2 teaspoons dried basil leaves
1 teaspoon salt

Crumble sausage into large skillet. Cook over medium heat until browned, stirring occasionally. Drain off any drippings. Whisk eggs in large bowl. Add sausage and remaining ingredients; mix well. Spoon into greased 13×9-inch baking dish. Cover; refrigerate 8 hours or overnight. Preheat oven to 350°F. Bake 60 to 70 minutes or until knife inserted near center comes out clean. Let stand 5 minutes before cutting into squares; serve hot. Refrigerate leftovers.

Makes 10 to 12 servings

Mexican Strata Olé

4 (6-inch) corn tortillas, halved, divided
1 cup chopped onion
½ cup chopped green bell pepper
1 clove garlic, crushed
1 teaspoon dried oregano leaves
½ teaspoon ground cumin
1 teaspoon margarine
1 cup dried kidney beans, cooked in
    unsalted water according to package
    directions
½ cup (2 ounces) shredded reduced-fat
    Cheddar cheese
1½ cups skim milk
1 cup EGG BEATERS® Healthy Real Egg
    Product
1 cup thick and chunky salsa

Arrange half of tortilla pieces on bottom of greased 12×8-inch baking dish; set aside.

In large nonstick skillet, over medium-high heat, sauté onion, bell pepper, garlic, oregano and cumin in margarine until tender; stir in beans. Spoon half of mixture over tortillas; repeat layers once. Sprinkle with cheese.

In medium bowl, combine milk and Egg Beaters®; pour evenly over cheese. Bake at 350°F for 40 minutes or until puffed and golden brown. Let stand 10 minutes before serving. Serve topped with salsa.

Makes 8 servings

Weekend Brunch Casserole

1 pound BOB EVANS FARMS® Original
    Recipe Roll Sausage
1 (8-ounce) can refrigerated crescent
    dinner rolls
2 cups (8 ounces) shredded mozzarella
    cheese
4 eggs, beaten
¾ cup milk
¼ teaspoon salt
⅛ teaspoon black pepper

Preheat oven to 425°F. Crumble sausage into medium
skillet. Cook over medium heat until browned, stirring
occasionally. Drain off any drippings. Line bottom of
greased 13×9-inch baking dish with crescent roll
dough, firmly pressing perforations to seal. Sprinkle
with sausage and cheese. Combine remaining
ingredients in medium bowl until blended; pour over
sausage. Bake 15 minutes or until set. Let stand
5 minutes before cutting into squares; serve hot.
Refrigerate leftovers. *Makes 6 to 8 servings*

Baked Ham & Cheese Monte Cristo

6 slices bread
2 cups (8 ounces) shredded Cheddar
   cheese
1 can (2.8 ounces) FRENCH'S® French
   Fried Onions
1 package (10 ounces) frozen broccoli
   spears, thawed, drained and cut into
   1-inch pieces
2 cups (10 ounces) cubed cooked ham
5 eggs
2 cups milk
½ teaspoon ground mustard
½ teaspoon seasoned salt
¼ teaspoon coarsely ground black pepper

Preheat oven to 325°F. Cut 3 bread slices into cubes; place in greased 12×8-inch baking dish. Top bread with *1 cup* cheese, *½ can* French Fried Onions, broccoli and ham. Cut remaining bread slices diagonally into halves. Arrange bread halves down center of casserole, overlapping slightly, crusted points all in same direction. In medium bowl, beat eggs, milk and seasonings; pour evenly over casserole. Bake, uncovered, at 325°F for 1 hour or until center is set. Top with remaining cheese and onions; bake, uncovered, 5 minutes or until onions are golden brown. Let stand 10 minutes before serving.

Makes 6 to 8 servings

Make-Ahead Breakfast Casserole

2½ cups seasoned croutons
1 pound BOB EVANS FARMS® Original
    Recipe Roll Sausage
4 eggs
2¼ cups milk
1 (10½-ounce) can condensed cream of
    mushroom soup
1 (10-ounce) package frozen chopped
    spinach, thawed and squeezed dry
1 (4-ounce) can mushrooms, drained and
    chopped
1 cup (4 ounces) shredded sharp Cheddar
    cheese
1 cup (4 ounces) shredded Monterey Jack
    cheese
¼ teaspoon dry mustard
    Picante sauce or salsa (optional)

Spread croutons on bottom of greased 13×9-inch
baking dish. Crumble sausage into medium skillet.
Cook over medium heat until browned, stirring
occasionally. Drain off any drippings. Spread over
croutons. Whisk eggs and milk in large bowl until
blended. Stir in soup, spinach, mushrooms, cheeses
and mustard. Pour egg mixture over sausage and
croutons. Refrigerate overnight. Preheat oven to 325°F.
Bake egg mixture 50 to 55 minutes or until set and
lightly browned on top. Serve hot with picante sauce, if
desired. Refrigerate leftovers.

Makes 10 to 12 servings

Sunrise Squares

1 **pound BOB EVANS FARMS® Original Recipe Roll Sausage**
2 **slices bread, cut into ½-inch cubes (about 2 cups)**
1 **cup (4 ounces) shredded sharp Cheddar cheese**
6 **eggs**
2 **cups milk**
½ **teaspoon salt**
½ **teaspoon dry mustard**

Preheat oven to 350°F. Crumble sausage into medium skillet. Cook over medium heat until browned, stirring occasionally. Drain off any drippings. Spread bread cubes in greased 11×7-inch baking dish; top with sausage and cheese. Whisk eggs, milk, salt and mustard until well blended; pour over cheese. Bake 30 to 40 minutes or until set. Let stand 5 minutes before cutting into squares; serve hot. Refrigerate leftovers.

Makes 6 servings

Tip: You can make this tasty meal ahead and refrigerate overnight before baking.

Spinach-Cheddar Squares

1½ cups EGG BEATERS® Healthy Real
      Egg Product
¾ cup skim milk
1 tablespoon dried onion flakes
1 tablespoon grated Parmesan cheese
¼ teaspoon garlic powder
⅛ teaspoon ground black pepper
⅛ cup plain dry bread crumbs
¾ cup shredded fat-free Cheddar cheese,
      divided
1 (10-ounce) package frozen chopped
      spinach, thawed and well drained
¼ cup diced pimentos

In medium bowl, combine Egg Beaters®, milk, onion
flakes, Parmesan cheese, garlic powder and pepper; set
aside.

Sprinkle bread crumbs evenly onto bottom of lightly
greased 8×8×2-inch baking dish. Top with ½ cup
Cheddar cheese and spinach. Pour egg mixture evenly
over spinach; top with remaining Cheddar cheese and
pimentos.

Bake at 350°F for 35 to 40 minutes or until knife
inserted into center comes out clean. Let stand 10
minutes before serving.   *Makes 4 servings*

Cheesy Country Spam™ Puff

  6 slices white bread, torn into small
     pieces
1¼ cups milk
  3 eggs
  1 tablespoon spicy mustard
  ½ teaspoon garlic powder
  ½ teaspoon paprika
  1 (12-ounce) can SPAM® Luncheon Meat,
     cubed
  2 cups (8 ounces) shredded sharp
     Cheddar cheese, divided
  ½ cup chopped onion
  ½ cup (2 ounces) shredded Monterey Jack
     cheese

Heat oven to 375°F. In large bowl, combine bread,
milk, eggs, mustard, garlic powder and paprika. Beat at
medium speed of electric mixer 1 minute or until
smooth. Stir in SPAM®, 1 cup Cheddar cheese and
onion. Pour into greased 12×8-inch baking dish. Bake
25 minutes. Top with remaining 1 cup Cheddar cheese
and Monterey Jack cheese. Bake 5 minutes longer or
until cheese is melted. Let stand 10 minutes before
serving.   *Makes 6 servings*

Asparagus-Swiss Souffle

¼ cup unsalted butter substitute
½ cup chopped yellow onion
¼ cup all-purpose flour
½ teaspoon salt
¼ teaspoon cayenne pepper
1 cup 2% low fat milk
1 cup (4 ounces) shredded ALPINE
     LACE® Reduced Fat Swiss Cheese
1 cup egg substitute *or* 4 large eggs
1 cup coarsely chopped fresh asparagus
     pieces, cooked, or frozen asparagus
     pieces, thawed and drained
3 large egg whites

1. Preheat the oven to 325°F. Spray a 1½-quart soufflé dish with nonstick cooking spray.

2. In a large saucepan, melt the butter over medium heat; add the onion and sauté for 5 minutes or until soft. Stir in the flour, salt and pepper and cook for 2 minutes or until bubbly. Add the milk and cook, stirring constantly, for 5 minutes or until the sauce thickens. Add the cheese and stir until melted.

3. In a small bowl, whisk the egg substitute (or the whole eggs). Whisk in a little of the hot cheese sauce, then return this egg mixture to the saucepan and whisk until well blended. Remove from the heat and fold in the drained asparagus.

4. In a medium-size bowl, using an electric mixer set on high, beat the egg whites until stiff peaks form. Fold the hot cheese sauce into the whites, then spoon into the soufflé dish.

5. Place the soufflé on a baking sheet and bake for 50 minutes or until golden brown and puffy.

Makes 8 servings

Ham & Cheese Grits Soufflé

    3 cups water
    ¾ cup quick-cooking grits
    ½ teaspoon salt
    ½ cup (2 ounces) shredded mozzarella
       cheese
    2 ounces ham, finely chopped
    2 tablespoons minced chives
    2 eggs, separated
       Dash hot pepper sauce

1. Preheat oven to 375°F. Grease 1½-quart soufflé dish or deep casserole.

2. Bring water to a boil in medium saucepan. Stir in grits and salt. Cook, stirring frequently, about 5 minutes or until thickened. Stir in cheese, ham, chives, egg yolks and hot pepper sauce.

3. In small clean bowl, beat egg whites until stiff but not dry; fold into grits mixture. Pour into prepared dish. Bake about 30 minutes or until puffed and golden. Serve immediately.   *Makes 4 to 6 servings*

Brunch Eggs Olé

8 eggs
½ cup all-purpose flour
1 teaspoon baking powder
¾ teaspoon salt
2 cups (8 ounces) shredded Monterey
    Jack cheese with jalapeño peppers
1½ cups (12 ounces) small curd cottage
    cheese
1 cup (4 ounces) shredded sharp Cheddar
    cheese
1 jalapeño pepper, seeded and chopped*
½ teaspoon hot pepper sauce
    Fresh Salsa (recipe follows)

1. Preheat oven to 350°F. Grease 9-inch square baking pan.

2. Beat eggs in large bowl at high speed with electric mixer 4 to 5 minutes or until slightly thickened and lemon colored.

3. Combine flour, baking powder and salt in small bowl. Stir flour mixture into eggs until blended.

4. Combine Monterey Jack cheese, cottage cheese, Cheddar cheese, jalapeño and pepper sauce in medium bowl; mix well. Fold into egg mixture until well blended. Pour into prepared pan.

5. Bake 45 to 50 minutes or until golden brown and firm in center. Let stand 10 minutes before cutting into squares. Serve with Fresh Salsa.

Makes 8 servings

*Jalapeño peppers can sting and irritate the skin; wear rubber gloves when handling peppers and do not touch eyes. Wash hands after handling.

Fresh Salsa

3   medium plum tomatoes, seeded and
      chopped
2   tablespoons chopped onion
1   small jalapeño pepper, stemmed, seeded
      and minced*
1   tablespoon chopped fresh cilantro
1   tablespoon lime juice
¼   teaspoon salt
⅛   teaspoon black pepper

Stir together tomatoes, onion, jalapeño pepper, cilantro, lime juice, salt and black pepper in small bowl. Refrigerate until ready to serve.

Makes 1 cup

*Jalapeño peppers can sting and irritate the skin; wear rubber gloves when handling peppers and do not touch eyes. Wash hands after handling.

Eggs Santa Fe

- **2 eggs**
- **½ cup GUILTLESS GOURMET® Black Bean Dip (mild or spicy)**
- **¼ cup GUILTLESS GOURMET® Salsa (mild, medium or hot)**
- **1 ounce (about 20) GUILTLESS GOURMET® Unsalted Baked Tortilla Chips**
- **2 tablespoons low fat sour cream**
- **1 teaspoon chopped fresh cilantro**
  Fresh cilantro sprigs (optional)

To poach eggs, bring water to a boil in small skillet over high heat; reduce heat to medium-low and maintain a simmer. Gently break eggs into water, being careful not to break yolks. Cover and simmer 5 minutes or until desired firmness.

Meanwhile, place bean dip in small microwave safe bowl or small saucepan. Microwave bean dip on HIGH (100% power) 2 to 3 minutes or heat over medium heat until warm. To serve, spread ¼ cup warm bean dip in center of serving plate; top with 1 poached egg and 2 tablespoons salsa. Arrange 10 tortilla chips around egg. Dollop with 1 tablespoon sour cream and sprinkle with ½ teaspoon chopped cilantro. Repeat with remaining ingredients. Garnish with cilantro sprigs, if desired. *Makes 2 servings*

Eggs Benedict Mousseline

6   ounces (1 carton) ALPINE LACE® Fat
    Free Cream Cheese with Garden
    Vegetables
¼   cup 2% low fat milk
1   tablespoon unsalted butter substitute
1   tablespoon fresh lemon juice
    Dash cayenne pepper
2   regular-size English muffins, split
4   thin slices (½ ounce each) ALPINE
    LACE® Boneless Cooked Ham,
    divided
1   teaspoon white vinegar
4   large eggs

1. Preheat the broiler. In a medium-size saucepan, heat the cheese, milk and butter over medium heat until the cheese is melted, then whisk in the lemon juice and pepper. Keep warm.

2. On a baking sheet, arrange the 4 muffin halves, split sides up. Broil for 1 minute or until golden brown; keep warm. In a large nonstick skillet, cook the ham over medium heat for 2 minutes. Place one slice of ham on each muffin half. Wipe out the skillet.

3. Fill the skillet two-thirds full with water. Add the vinegar and bring to a simmer over medium heat. Break each egg into a saucer, then slide it into the water. Spoon the water gently over the eggs for 3 minutes or until they are the way you like them. Using a slotted spoon, place 1 egg on each muffin, ladle some sauce over the top and serve.   *Makes 4 servings*

Ham and Egg Enchiladas

2 tablespoons butter or margarine
1 small red bell pepper, chopped
3 green onions with tops, sliced
½ cup diced ham
8 eggs
8 (8-inch) flour tortillas
2 cups (8 ounces) shredded Colby Jack cheese or Monterey Jack cheese with jalapeño peppers, divided
1 can (10 ounces) enchilada sauce
½ cup prepared salsa
Sliced avocado, fresh cilantro and red pepper slices for garnish

1. Preheat oven to 350°F.

2. Melt butter in large nonstick skillet over medium heat. Add bell pepper and onions; cook and stir 2 minutes. Add ham; cook and stir 1 minute.

3. Lightly beat eggs with wire whisk in medium bowl. Add eggs to skillet; cook until set but still soft, stirring occasionally.

4. Spoon about ⅓ cup egg mixture evenly down center of each tortilla; top with 1 tablespoon cheese. Roll tortillas up and place seam side down in shallow 11×7-inch baking dish.

5. Combine enchilada sauce and salsa in small bowl; pour evenly over enchiladas.

6. Cover enchiladas with foil; bake 20 minutes. Uncover; sprinkle with remaining cheese. Continue baking 10 minutes or until enchiladas are hot and cheese is melted. Garnish, if desired. Serve immediately. *Makes 4 servings*

Acapulco Eggs

> 3 corn tortillas, cut into 2-inch strips
> 3 tablespoons butter or margarine
> ½ cup chopped onion
> 1½ cups DEL MONTE® Thick & Chunky Salsa, Mild
> 1 cup cooked ham, cut into thin strips, or shredded cooked turkey
> ½ cup green bell pepper strips
> 6 eggs, beaten
> ¾ cup shredded Monterey Jack cheese

1. Cook tortilla strips in butter until golden. Remove and set aside.

2. Cook onion in same skillet until tender. Stir in salsa, meat and green pepper; heat through.

3. Reduce heat to low; add tortillas and eggs. Cover and cook 4 to 6 minutes or until eggs are set.

4. Sprinkle with cheese; cover and cook 1 minute or until cheese is melted. Garnish with chopped cilantro or parsley, if desired. *Makes 4 to 6 servings*

Brunch Rice

1 teaspoon margarine
¾ cup shredded carrots
¾ cup diced green pepper
¾ cup (about 3 ounces) sliced fresh
    mushrooms
6 egg whites, beaten
2 eggs, beaten
½ cup skim milk
½ teaspoon salt
¼ teaspoon ground black pepper
3 cups cooked brown rice
½ cup (2 ounces) shredded Cheddar
    cheese
6 corn tortillas, warmed (optional)

Melt margarine in large skillet over medium-high heat.
Add carrots, green pepper and mushrooms; cook and
stir 2 minutes. Combine egg whites, eggs, milk, salt
and black pepper in small bowl. Reduce heat to
medium; pour egg white mixture over vegetables in
skillet. Continue cooking 2 minutes, stirring
occasionally. Add rice and cheese; stir to gently
separate grains. Cook 2 minutes or until rice is heated
through and cheese is melted. Spoon mixture into
warmed corn tortillas, if desired. Serve immediately.

Makes 6 servings

Favorite recipe from **USA Rice Council**

Huevos Con Arroz

1 package (6.8 ounces) RICE-A-RONI®
  Spanish Rice
2 cups chopped tomatoes
4 eggs
½ cup (2 ounces) shredded Cheddar
  cheese or Monterey Jack cheese
2 tablespoons chopped cilantro or parsley
¼ cup salsa or picante sauce (optional)

1. Prepare Rice-A-Roni® mix as package directs, substituting fresh tomatoes for 1 can (14½ ounces) tomatoes. Bring to a boil over high heat. Cover; reduce heat. Simmer 20 minutes.

2. Make 4 round indentations in rice with back of large spoon. Break 1 egg into each indentation. Cover; cook over low heat 5 to 7 minutes or until eggs are cooked to desired doneness.

3. Sprinkle with cheese and cilantro. Serve topped with salsa, if desired. *Makes 4 servings*

Creamy Chicken & Vegetables with Puff Pastry

2 whole chicken breasts, split (about 2
    pounds)
1 medium onion, sliced
4 carrots, coarsely chopped, divided
4 ribs celery with leaves, cut into 1-inch
    pieces, divided
1 frozen puff pastry sheet, thawed
2 tablespoons butter or margarine
1 medium onion, chopped
½ pound fresh mushrooms, sliced
½ cup all-purpose flour
1 teaspoon dried basil leaves
1 teaspoon salt
¼ to ½ teaspoon white pepper
1 cup milk
1 cup frozen peas, thawed

1. To make chicken stock, place chicken, sliced onion, *⅓ each* of carrots and celery in Dutch oven. Add enough cold water to cover. Cover and bring to a boil over medium heat. Reduce heat to low. Simmer 5 to 7 minutes or until chicken is no longer pink in center.

2. Remove chicken; cool. Strain stock through large sieve lined with several layers of dampened cheesecloth; discard vegetables. Refrigerate stock; skim off any fat that forms on top. Measure 2 cups stock.

3. When chicken is cool enough to handle, remove skin and bones; discard. Cut chicken into bite-sized pieces. Set aside.

4. Place remaining carrots, celery and enough water to cover in medium saucepan. Cover; bring to a boil. Reduce heat to medium-low; simmer 8 minutes or until vegetables are crisp-tender. Set aside.

5. Preheat oven to 400°F. Roll puff pastry out on lightly floured surface to 12×8-inch rectangle. Place on ungreased baking sheet; bake 15 minutes. Set aside.

6. Melt butter in large saucepan over medium-high heat. Add chopped onion and mushrooms; cook and stir 5 minutes or until tender. Stir in flour, basil, salt and pepper. Slowly pour in reserved 2 cups chicken stock and milk. Cook until mixture begins to boil. Cook 1 minute longer, stirring constantly.

7. Stir in peas, reserved chicken, carrots and celery. Cook until heated through. Pour mixture into 12×8-inch baking dish; top with hot puff pastry. Bake 5 minutes until puff pastry is brown.

Makes 6 servings

Brown Rice, Mushroom and Ham Hash

1 tablespoon olive oil
2 cups (about 8 ounces) sliced fresh
    mushrooms
1 small onion, minced
1 clove garlic, minced
3 cups cooked brown rice
1 cup (6 ounces) diced turkey ham
½ cup chopped walnuts (optional)
¼ cup snipped parsley
1 tablespoon white wine vinegar
1 tablespoon Dijon mustard
¼ teaspoon ground black pepper

Heat oil in Dutch oven or large saucepan over
medium-low heat until hot. Add mushrooms, onion
and garlic; cook until tender. Stir in rice, ham,
walnuts, parsley, vinegar, mustard and pepper; cook,
stirring until thoroughly heated.

Makes 8 servings

To microwave: Combine oil, mushrooms, onion and
garlic in 2- to 3-quart microwavable baking dish. Cook
on HIGH 3 to 4 minutes. Stir in rice, ham, walnuts,
parsley, vinegar, mustard and pepper. Cook on HIGH
3 to 4 minutes, stirring after 2 minutes, or until
thoroughly heated.

Favorite recipe from **USA Rice Council**

Mushroom & Onion Egg Bake

1 tablespoon vegetable oil
4 green onions, chopped
4 ounces mushrooms, sliced
1 cup low-fat cottage cheese
1 cup sour cream
6 eggs
2 tablespoons all-purpose flour
¼ teaspoon salt
⅛ teaspoon freshly ground pepper
   Dash hot pepper sauce

1. Preheat oven to 350°F. Grease shallow 1-quart baking dish.

2. Heat oil in medium skillet over medium heat. Add onions and mushrooms; cook until tender. Set aside.

3. In blender or food processor, process cottage cheese until almost smooth. Add sour cream, eggs, flour, salt, pepper and pepper sauce; process until combined. Stir in onions and mushrooms. Pour into prepared baking dish. Bake about 40 minutes or until knife inserted near center comes out clean.

Makes about 6 servings

Sunrise French Toast

2 cups cholesterol-free egg substitute
½ cup evaporated skim milk
1 teaspoon grated orange peel
1 teaspoon vanilla
¼ teaspoon ground cinnamon
1 jar (10 ounces) no-sugar-added orange
    marmalade
1 loaf (1 pound) Italian bread, cut into
    ½-inch thick slices (about 20 slices)
    Nonstick cooking spray
    Powdered sugar
    Maple-flavored syrup (optional)

1. Preheat oven to 400°F. Combine egg substitute, milk, orange peel, vanilla and cinnamon in medium bowl. Set aside.

2. Spread 1 tablespoon marmalade over 1 bread slice to within ½ inch of edge. Top with another bread slice. Repeat with remaining marmalade and bread.

3. Spray griddle or large skillet with cooking spray; heat over medium heat until hot. Dip sandwiches in egg substitute mixture. Do not soak. Cook sandwiches in batches 2 to 3 minutes on each side or until golden brown.

4. Transfer sandwiches to 15×10-inch jelly roll pan. Bake 10 to 12 minutes or until sides are sealed. Dust with powdered sugar and serve with syrup.

Makes 5 servings

Apple-Potato Pancakes

1¼ cups unpeeled, finely chopped apples
1 cup peeled, grated potatoes
½ cup Mott's Natural Apple Sauce
½ cup all-purpose flour
2 egg whites
1 teaspoon salt
   Additional MOTT'S® Natural Apple
   Sauce or apple slices (optional)

1. Preheat oven to 475°F. Spray cookie sheet with nonstick cooking spray.

2. In medium bowl, combine apples, potatoes, ½ cup apple sauce, flour, egg whites and salt.

3. Spray large nonstick skillet with nonstick cooking spray; heat over medium heat until hot. Drop rounded tablespoonfuls of batter 2 inches apart into skillet. Cook 2 to 3 minutes on each side or until lightly browned. Place pancakes on prepared cookie sheet.

4. Bake 10 to 15 minutes or until crisp. Serve with additional apple sauce or apple slices, if desired. Refrigerate leftovers. *Makes 12 servings*

Dinner

EXPRESS

Eggplant Parmesan

½ cup vegetable oil, divided
1½ pounds (1 medium) eggplant, peeled, cut into ½-inch-thick slices
1¾ cups (15-ounce container) ricotta cheese
2 cups (17-ounce can) CONTADINA® Dalla Casa Buitoni Country Italian Cooking Sauce with Three Cheeses & Herbs
½ cup CONTADINA® Dalla Casa Buitoni Seasoned Bread Crumbs
¼ cup grated Parmesan cheese

HEAT 2 tablespoons oil in large skillet over medium-high heat. Add a few slices eggplant; cook 2 to 3 minutes on each side or until tender. Drain on paper towels. Repeat with remaining oil and eggplant.

PLACE half of eggplant slices in greased 12×7-inch baking dish. Spread half of ricotta cheese over eggplant. Pour half of cooking sauce over ricotta cheese. Combine bread crumbs and Parmesan cheese in small bowl; sprinkle half over cooking sauce. Repeat layers.

BAKE in 350°F oven 25 to 30 minutes or until sauce is bubbly.   *Makes 6 servings*

Chicken Divan

¾ pound fresh broccoli, cut into flowerets
     or 1 package (10 ounces) frozen
     broccoli flowerets
2 cups shredded cooked chicken
1 cup prepared HIDDEN VALLEY
     RANCH® Original Ranch® salad
     dressing
1 tablespoon grated Parmesan cheese
     Cherry tomatoes

Preheat oven to 350°F. In medium saucepan, cook broccoli in boiling water to cover until tender, about 4 minutes. Drain thoroughly; place in shallow baking dish. Top with chicken and salad dressing. Sprinkle with Parmesan cheese. Cover loosely with foil; bake until heated through, about 15 minutes. Garnish with cherry tomatoes.   *Makes 4 servings*

Florentine Chicken

2 boxes (10 ounces each) BIRDS EYE®
     frozen Chopped Spinach
1 package (1¼ ounces) hollandaise sauce
     mix
½ teaspoon Tabasco® pepper sauce or to
     taste
⅓ cup shredded Cheddar cheese, divided
1½ cups cooked chicken, cut into cubes

• Preheat oven to 350°F.

• Cook spinach according to package directions; drain. Prepare hollandaise sauce according to package directions.

• Blend spinach, hollandaise sauce, Tabasco® sauce and half of cheese. Pour into 9×9-inch baking dish; top with chicken.

• Sprinkle remaining cheese on top. Bake 10 to 12 minutes or until heated through.

Makes 4 servings

Potato Tuna au Gratin

1 **package (5 or 6 ounces) Cheddar cheese au gratin potatoes**
1 **can (12 ounces) STARKIST® Solid White or Chunk Light Tuna, drained and chunked**
¼ **cup chopped onion**
1 **package (16 ounces) frozen broccoli cuts, cooked and drained**
¾ **cup shredded Cheddar cheese**
¼ **cup bread crumbs**

Prepare potatoes according to package directions. While potatoes are standing, stir in tuna and onion. Arrange cooked broccoli in bottom of lightly greased 11×7-inch baking dish. Pour tuna-potato mixture over broccoli; top with cheese. Broil 3 to 4 minutes or until cheese is bubbly. Sprinkle bread crumbs over top.

Makes 6 servings

Tuna Feast

2 cans (15 ounces each) asparagus
   spears, well-drained
2 cans (6 ounces each) tuna, drained and
   flaked
1 medium onion, chopped (optional)
2 cups prepared HIDDEN VALLEY
   RANCH® Reduced Calorie Original
   Ranch® salad dressing
2 cups shredded Cheddar cheese
1 to 1½ cups herb-flavored croutons

Preheat oven to 350°F. Butter 3-quart casserole dish.
Arrange asparagus spears in dish; top with tuna and
onion. Cover with salad dressing; sprinkle with cheese
and croutons. Bake until thoroughly heated and cheese
is melted, about 15 minutes.

Makes 6 to 8 servings

Sausage & Biscuits Strata

1 pound BOB EVANS FARMS® Original
   Recipe Roll Sausage
6 prepared biscuits, split and buttered
1 cup (4 ounces) shredded Cheddar
   cheese
8 eggs
1½ cups milk
½ cup pancake syrup

Crumble sausage into large skillet. Cook over medium heat until browned, stirring occasionally. Drain off any drippings. Spoon into greased 13×9-inch baking dish; top with biscuits, split sides down, and sprinkle with cheese. Whisk eggs, milk and pancake syrup in large bowl until blended. Pour over biscuits. Cover; refrigerate 8 hours or overnight. Preheat oven to 350°F. Bake 60 to 70 minutes or until knife inserted near center comes out clean. Let stand 5 minutes before cutting into squares; serve hot. Refrigerate leftovers.   *Makes 8 servings*

Stuffed Green Peppers

6 medium to large green bell peppers
1 pound BOB EVANS FARMS® Original
    Recipe Roll Sausage
2 cups tomato sauce
2 cups water
1 small onion, chopped
1 cup uncooked rice
    Sliced green onion (optional)

Preheat oven to 350°F. Slice off tops from peppers;
scrape out centers to remove seeds and membranes.
Combine all remaining ingredients except green onion
in medium bowl; mix well. Evenly stuff peppers with
sausage mixture. Place in lightly greased deep 3-quart
casserole dish. Bake, covered, 20 minutes. Uncover;
bake 5 to 10 minutes more or until peppers are fork-
tender and filling is set. Garnish with green onion, if
desired. Serve hot. Refrigerate leftovers.

Makes 6 servings

Tip: For a pretty presentation, slice 6 small peppers
lengthwise in half through stem; scrape out centers to
remove seeds and membranes. Proceed as directed,
serving 2 halves to each guest.

Chicken Parmesan Noodle Bake

1 package (12 ounces) extra wide noodles
4 half boneless chicken breasts, skinned
½ teaspoon rosemary, crushed
2 cans (14½ ounces each) DEL MONTE®
  FreshCut™ Diced Tomatoes with
  Basil, Garlic & Oregano Italian
  Recipe Stewed Tomatoes
½ cup (2 ounces) shredded mozzarella
  cheese
¼ cup (1 ounce) grated Parmesan cheese

1. Preheat oven to 450°F.

2. Cook noodles according to package directions; drain. Keep warm.

3. Meanwhile, sprinkle chicken with rosemary; season with salt and pepper, if desired. Arrange chicken in shallow baking dish. Bake, uncovered, 20 minutes or until chicken is no longer pink in center. Drain; remove chicken from dish.

4. Drain tomatoes, reserving liquid. In large bowl, toss reserved liquid with noodles; place in baking dish. Top with chicken and tomatoes. Sprinkle with cheeses.

5. Bake 10 minutes or until heated through. Sprinkle with additional Parmesan cheese, if desired.

Makes 4 servings

Baked Spam® & Tortellini Casserole

1   (30-ounce) jar spaghetti sauce
1   (12-ounce) can SPAM® Luncheon Meat,
      cubed
1   (10-ounce) package refrigerated cheese
      tortellini
½   cup chopped onion
1   cup (4 ounces) shredded mozzarella
      cheese

Heat oven to 375°F. In 2½-quart casserole combine all
ingredients except cheese; mix gently. Bake, covered,
stirring halfway through baking, 50 to 60 minutes or
until tortellini are tender. During last 5 minutes of
baking, uncover and top with cheese.

Makes 6 servings

Ziti & Tuna Bake

6   ounces ziti pasta, cooked and drained
1   jar (15 ounces) spaghetti sauce with
      mushrooms
1   can (9 ounces) STARKIST® Tuna,
      drained and broken into chunks
½   cup sliced pitted ripe olives
1   cup shredded low fat mozzarella cheese
      Chopped parsley

In large bowl, toss together cooked pasta, spaghetti sauce, tuna, olives and ½ of the mozzarella. Transfer mixture to a 10×6×2-inch microwavable casserole. Cover with waxed paper; microcook on HIGH power for 9 minutes, rotating dish ¼ turn every 3 minutes. Sprinkle remaining cheese over casserole. Let stand, covered, 2 minutes to melt cheese. Sprinkle with parsley. *Makes 4 servings*

Spam® Cheesy Broccoli Bake

1 (10-ounce) package frozen chopped broccoli
1 (10¾-ounce) can Cheddar cheese soup
½ cup sour cream
1 (12-ounce) can SPAM® Luncheon Meat, cubed
1½ cups cooked white rice
½ cup buttered bread crumbs

Heat oven to 350°F. Cook broccoli according to package directions. Drain well. In medium bowl, combine soup and sour cream. Add broccoli, SPAM® and rice to soup mixture. Spoon into 1½-quart casserole. Sprinkle with bread crumbs. Bake 30 to 35 minutes or until thoroughly heated.

Makes 4 to 6 servings

Italian Pasta Bake

1 **pound ground beef**
5 **cups cooked pasta**
1 **jar (30 ounces) spaghetti sauce**
½ **cup KRAFT® 100% Grated Parmesan Cheese**
2 **cups (8 ounces) KRAFT® Natural Shredded Low Moisture Part Skim Mozzarella Cheese**

COOK ground beef in large skillet and drain.

STIR in pasta, spaghetti sauce and Parmesan cheese. Spoon into 13×9-inch baking dish.

TOP with mozzarella cheese. Bake at 375°F for 20 minutes. *Makes 4 servings*

Spicy Quick and Easy Chili

1 **pound ground beef**
1 **large clove garlic, minced**
1 **can (15¼ ounces) DEL MONTE® FreshCut™ Golden Sweet Whole Kernel Corn, drained**
1 **can (16 ounces) kidney beans, drained**
1½ **cups DEL MONTE® Thick & Chunky Salsa, Mild, Medium or Hot**
1 **can (4 ounces) diced green chiles, undrained**

1. Brown meat in large saucepan with garlic; drain.

2. Add remaining ingredients. Simmer, uncovered, 10 minutes, stirring occasionally. Garnish with green onions, if desired.   *Makes 4 servings*

Mexicali Chicken Stew

  1 **package (1¼ ounces) taco seasoning, divided**
 12 **ounces boneless skinless chicken thighs**
  2 **cans (14½ ounces each) stewed tomatoes with onions, celery and green peppers**
  1 **package (9 ounces) frozen green beans**
  1 **package (10 ounces) frozen corn**
  4 **cups tortilla chips**

1. Place half of taco seasoning in small bowl. Cut chicken thighs into 1-inch pieces; coat with taco seasoning.

2. Coat large nonstick skillet with nonstick cooking spray. Cook and stir chicken 5 minutes over medium heat. Add tomatoes, beans, corn and remaining taco seasoning; bring to a boil. Reduce heat to medium-low; simmer 10 minutes. Top with tortilla chips before serving.   *Makes 4 servings*

Ham and Cauliflower Chowder

1 bag (16 ounces) BIRDS EYE® frozen
    Cauliflower
2 cans (10¾ ounces each) cream of
    mushroom or cream of celery soup
2½ cups milk or water
½ pound ham, cubed
⅓ cup shredded Colby cheese (optional)

• Cook cauliflower according to package directions.

• Combine cauliflower, soup, milk and ham in
saucepan; mix well.

• Cook over medium heat 4 to 6 minutes, stirring
occasionally. Top individual servings with cheese.

Makes 4 to 6 servings

Country Chicken Pot Pie

1 package (1.8 ounces) white sauce mix
2¼ cups milk
2 to 3 cups diced cooked chicken
3 cups BIRDS EYE® frozen Mixed
    Vegetables
1½ cups seasoned croutons

• Prepare white sauce mix with milk in large skillet
according to package directions.

• Add chicken and vegetables. Bring to a boil over
medium-high heat; cook 3 minutes or until heated
through, stirring occasionally.

• Top with croutons; cover and let stand 5 minutes.
Makes about 4 servings

Stir-Fry Beef Vegetable Soup

1 **pound boneless beef steak, such as
  sirloin or round steak**
2 **teaspoons dark sesame oil, divided**
3 **cans (about 14 ounces each)
  reduced-sodium beef broth**
1 **package (16 ounces) frozen stir-fry
  vegetables**
3 **green onions, thinly sliced**
¼ **cup stir-fry sauce**

1. Slice beef across grain into ⅛-inch-thick strips; cut strips into bite-size pieces.

2. Heat Dutch oven over high heat. Add 1 teaspoon oil and tilt pan to coat bottom. Add half the beef in single layer; cook 1 minute, without stirring, until slightly browned on bottom. Turn and brown other side about 1 minute. Remove beef from pan with slotted spoon; set aside. Repeat with remaining 1 teaspoon oil and beef; set aside.

3. Add beef broth to Dutch oven; cover and bring to a boil over high heat. Add vegetables; reduce heat to medium-high and simmer 3 to 5 minutes or until heated through. Add beef, green onions and stir-fry sauce; simmer 1 minute more.   *Makes 6 servings*

Breakfast Pizza

1 **can (10 ounces) refrigerated ready-to-use pizza dough**
1 **package (7 ounces) pre-browned fully cooked sausage patties, thawed**
3 **eggs**
½ **cup milk**
1 **teaspoon dried Italian seasoning**
2 **cups (8 ounces) shredded pizza-style cheese**

1. Preheat oven to 425°F. For crust, unroll pizza dough and pat onto bottom and up side of greased 12-inch pizza pan. Bake 5 minutes or until set, but not browned.

2. While crust is baking, cut sausages into ½-inch pieces. Whisk together eggs, milk and Italian seasoning in medium bowl until well blended. Season to taste with salt and pepper.

3. Spoon sausage over crust; sprinkle with cheese. Carefully pour egg mixture over sausage and cheese. Bake 15 to 20 minutes or until egg mixture is set and crust is golden. *Makes 6 servings*

Italian Omelet

¼ cup chopped tomato
¼ cup (1 ounce) shredded part-skim
    mozzarella cheese
¼ teaspoon dried basil leaves
¼ teaspoon dried oregano leaves
1 teaspoon margarine
1 cup EGG BEATERS® Healthy Real Egg
    Product
    Chopped fresh parsley, for garnish

In small bowl, combine tomato, cheese, basil and oregano; set aside.

In 8-inch nonstick skillet, over medium heat, melt margarine. Pour Egg Beaters® into skillet. Cook, lifting edges to allow uncooked portion to flow underneath. When almost set, spoon tomato mixture over half of omelet. Fold other half over tomato mixture; cover and continue to cook 1 to 2 minutes. Slide onto serving plate. Garnish with parsley.   *Makes 2 servings*

Zucchini Omelet

6 eggs
¾ cup prepared HIDDEN VALLEY
    RANCH® Original Ranch® salad
    dressing
½ pound sliced zucchini
3 tablespoons butter or margarine
1 medium tomato, diced
    Fresh chives or parsley

In medium bowl, beat eggs with ¼ cup of the salad
dressing. In medium skillet, sauté zucchini in 1
tablespoon of the butter. Add tomato and heat through;
keep warm. For each omelet, melt 1 tablespoon of the
butter in skillet. Add ½ of egg mixture and cook over
medium heat until set but not dry; remove from heat.
Fill center of omelet with zucchini mixture; fold over
and turn onto warmed platter. Top each omelet with ½
of remaining ½ cup dressing. Garnish with chives.

Makes 4 servings

Note: If preferred, substitute 1 package (10 ounces)
frozen mixed vegetables for fresh zucchini and tomato.

Potato & Onion Frittata

1 small baking potato, peeled, halved and
    sliced ⅛-inch thick (about ½ cup)
¼ cup chopped onion
1 clove garlic, minced
    Dash ground black pepper
1 tablespoon margarine
1 cup EGG BEATERS® Healthy Real Egg
    Product

In 8-inch nonstick skillet, over medium-high heat,
sauté potato, onion, garlic and pepper in margarine
until tender. Pour Egg Beaters® evenly into skillet over
potato mixture. Cook without stirring 5 to 6 minutes
or until cooked on bottom and almost set on top.
Carefully turn Frittata; cook 1 to 2 minutes more or
until done. Slide onto serving platter; cut into wedges
to serve.   *Makes 2 servings*

Vegetable Frittata

2 tablespoons butter or margarine
1 bag (16 ounces) BIRDS EYE® frozen
   Farm Fresh Mixtures Broccoli, Corn
   and Red Peppers
8 eggs
½ cup water
1 tablespoon Tabasco® pepper sauce
¾ teaspoon salt

• Melt butter in 12-inch nonstick skillet over medium heat. Add vegetables; cook and stir 3 minutes.

• Lightly beat eggs, water, Tabasco® sauce and salt.

• Pour egg mixture over vegetables in skillet. Cover and cook 10 to 15 minutes or until eggs are set.

• To serve, cut into wedges.

Makes about 4 servings

Spambled™ Egg Muffins

1 (12-ounce) can SPAM® Luncheon Meat
4 eggs, beaten
4 English muffins, split and toasted
   Butter or margarine
4 slices American cheese

Slice SPAM® into 4 square slices. In large skillet over medium heat, sauté SPAM® until lightly browned. Remove from skillet; set aside.

In same skillet, scramble eggs. Spread English muffins lightly with butter. Layer scrambled eggs, SPAM® slice and cheese slice on bottom half of each English muffin. Cover with top half of each muffin. Heat in microwave 30 seconds or in conventional oven 1 to 2 minutes or until cheese is melted. *Makes 4 servings*

Huevos Rancheros

- 1 cup GUILTLESS GOURMET® Salsa (mild, medium or hot)
- 2 eggs
- 2 corn tortillas (6 inches each)
- 2 tablespoons low fat sour cream
- 1 tablespoon chopped fresh cilantro

Bring salsa to a boil in small nonstick skillet over medium heat. Gently break eggs into salsa, being careful not to break yolks. Reduce heat to medium-low; cover and simmer 5 minutes or to desired firmness.

Meanwhile, to soften tortillas, wrap in damp paper towel. Microwave on HIGH (100% power) 20 seconds. Or, to soften tortillas in oven, preheat oven to 300°F. Wrap tortillas in foil. Bake 10 minutes. To serve, arrange 1 tortilla on serving plate; top with 1 egg and half the salsa. Dollop with 1 tablespoon sour cream and sprinkle with ½ tablespoon cilantro. Repeat with remaining ingredients. *Makes 2 servings*

Breakfast Hash

1 **pound BOB EVANS FARMS® Special**
   Seasonings or Sage Roll Sausage
2 **cups chopped potatoes**
¼ **cup chopped red and/or green bell**
   peppers
2 **tablespoons chopped onion**
6 **eggs**
2 **tablespoons milk**

Crumble sausage into large skillet. Add potatoes, peppers and onion. Cook over low heat until sausage is browned and potatoes are fork-tender, stirring occasionally. Drain off any drippings. Whisk eggs and milk in small bowl until blended. Add to sausage mixture; scramble until eggs are set but not dry. Serve hot. Refrigerate leftovers.   *Makes 6 to 8 servings*

Beef Teriyaki Stir-Fry

1 cup uncooked rice
1 pound beef sirloin, thinly sliced
½ cup teriyaki marinade, divided
2 tablespoons vegetable oil, divided
1 medium onion, halved and sliced
2 cups frozen green beans, rinsed and
    drained

1. Cook rice according to package directions, omitting salt.

2. Combine beef and ¼ cup marinade in medium bowl; set aside.

3. Heat ½ tablespoon oil in wok or large skillet over medium-high heat until hot. Add onion; stir-fry 3 to 4 minutes or until crisp-tender. Remove from wok to medium bowl.

4. Heat ½ tablespoon oil in wok until hot. Stir-fry beans 3 minutes or until crisp-tender and hot. Drain off excess liquid. Add beans to onion in bowl.

5. Heat remaining 1 tablespoon oil in wok until hot. Drain beef, discarding marinade. Stir-fry beef about 3 minutes or until browned. Stir in vegetables and remaining ¼ cup marinade; cook and stir 1 minute or until heated through. Serve with rice.

Makes 4 servings

Sesame Pork with Broccoli

2 **tablespoons sesame seeds**
1 **to 2 tablespoons peanut or vegetable oil**
1 **pound boneless pork, cut into thin
      strips**
4 **cups BIRDS EYE® frozen Broccoli Cuts**
⅓ **cup prepared stir-fry sauce**

• Stir sesame seeds in large skillet over high heat 1 to 2 minutes or until golden brown. Remove and reserve.

• Heat 1 tablespoon oil in same skillet over high heat. Add half the pork; cook and stir until browned. Push to side of skillet and add remaining pork. Cook and stir until browned, adding additional oil if necessary.

• Add broccoli and stir-fry sauce; cover and cook 5 minutes.

• Toss with reserved sesame seeds.

Makes about 4 servings

Shrimp and Vegetables with Lo Mein Noodles

2 **tablespoons vegetable oil**
1 **pound medium shrimp, peeled**
2 **packages (21 ounces each) frozen
  lo mein stir-fry mix with sauce**
¼ **cup peanuts**
  Fresh cilantro
1 **small wedge cabbage**

1. Heat oil in wok or large skillet over medium-high heat until hot. Add shrimp; stir-fry 3 minutes or until shrimp are pink and opaque. Remove from wok to medium bowl. Set aside.

2. Remove sauce packet from stir-fry mix. Add frozen vegetables and noodles to wok; stir in sauce. Cover and cook 7 to 8 minutes, stirring frequently.

3. While vegetable mixture is cooking, chop peanuts and enough cilantro to measure 2 tablespoons. Shred cabbage.

4. Stir shrimp, peanuts and cilantro into vegetable mixture; heat through. Serve immediately with cabbage. *Makes 6 servings*

Sweet & Sour Stir-Fry

1   tablespoon vegetable oil
½   pound boneless chicken breast or beef,
      cut into thin strips
1   bag (16 ounces) BIRDS EYE® frozen
      Farm Fresh Mixtures Sugar Snap
      Stir-Fry
1   tablespoon water
½   cup prepared sweet & sour sauce

• Heat oil in large skillet or wok. Stir-fry chicken until cooked through.

• Add vegetables and water; cover and cook 5 to 7 minutes over medium-high heat.

• Stir in sweet & sour sauce; heat through.

Makes 3 to 4 servings

Chicken and Asparagus Stir-Fry

1 **cup uncooked rice**
2 **tablespoons vegetable oil, divided**
1 **pound boneless skinless chicken breast, cut into ½-inch-wide strips**
2 **medium red bell peppers, cut into thin strips**
½ **pound fresh asparagus, cut diagonally into 1-inch pieces**
½ **cup bottled stir-fry sauce**

1. Cook rice according to package directions. Set aside.

2. Heat 1 tablespoon oil in wok or large skillet over medium-high heat until hot. Stir-fry chicken 3 to 4 minutes or until chicken is no longer pink in center. Remove from wok; set aside.

3. Heat remaining 1 tablespoon oil in wok until hot. Stir-fry bell peppers and asparagus 1 minute; reduce heat to medium. Cover and cook 2 minutes or until vegetables are crisp-tender, stirring once or twice.

4. Stir in chicken and sauce; heat through. Serve immediately with rice.   *Makes 4 servings*

Asian Chicken and Noodles

1 package (3 ounces) chicken flavor
   instant ramen noodles
1 bag (16 ounces) BIRDS EYE® frozen
   Farm Fresh Mixtures Broccoli,
   Carrots and Water Chestnuts*
1 tablespoon vegetable oil
1 pound boneless skinless chicken
   breasts, cut into thin strips
¼ cup stir-fry sauce

• Reserve seasoning packet from noodles.

• Bring 2 cups water to boil in large saucepan. Add noodles and vegetables. Cook 3 minutes, stirring occasionally; drain.

• Meanwhile, heat oil in large nonstick skillet over medium-high heat. Add chicken; cook and stir until browned, about 8 minutes.

• Stir in noodles, vegetables, stir-fry sauce and reserved seasoning packet; heat through.

Makes about 4 servings

*Or, substitute 1 bag (16 ounces) BIRDS EYE® frozen Broccoli Cuts.

Beef & Broccoli Pepper Steak

- 1 tablespoon margarine or butter
- 1 pound well-trimmed top round steak, cut into thin strips
- 1 package (6.8 ounces) RICE-A-RONI® Beef Flavor
- 2 cups broccoli florets
- ½ cup red or green bell pepper strips
- 1 small onion, thinly sliced

1. In large skillet, melt margarine over medium heat. Add meat; sauté just until browned.

2. Remove from skillet; set aside. Keep warm.

3. In same skillet, prepare Rice-A-Roni Mix as package directs; simmer 10 minutes. Add meat and remaining ingredients; simmer an additional 10 minutes or until most of liquid is absorbed and vegetables are crisp-tender. *Makes 4 servings*

Southwestern Skillet Dinner

1   **pound ground beef**
2   **teaspoons chili powder**
1   **jar (16 ounces) thick and chunky salsa**
1½ **cups BIRDS EYE® frozen Corn**
¾   **cup shredded Cheddar cheese**

• Cook ground beef in large skillet over high heat until well browned, about 8 minutes; drain. Stir in chili powder; cook 1 minute.

• Add salsa and corn; bring to boil. Reduce heat to medium; cover and cook 4 minutes.

• Sprinkle with cheese; cover and cook until cheese melts.   *Makes about 4 servings*

Ham & Potato Scallop

1   **package (5 ounces) scalloped potatoes plus ingredients as package directs**
1   **bag (16 ounces) BIRDS EYE® frozen Broccoli Cuts**
½   **pound cooked ham, cut into ½-inch cubes**
½   **cup shredded Cheddar cheese (optional)**

• Prepare potatoes according to package directions for stove-top method, adding broccoli and ham when adding milk and butter.

• Stir in cheese just before serving.

Makes 4 servings

New Orleans Rice and Sausage

½ pound smoked sausage, cut into slices*
1¾ cups uncooked instant rice
1 can (14½ ounces) stewed tomatoes,
     Cajun- or Italian-style
¾ cup water
     Dash hot pepper sauce, or to taste
1 bag (16 ounces) BIRDS EYE® frozen
     Farm Fresh Mixtures Broccoli, Corn
     and Red Peppers

• Heat sausage in large skillet 2 to 3 minutes.

• Add rice, tomatoes, water and hot pepper sauce;
mix well.

• Add vegetables; mix well. Cover and cook over
medium heat 5 to 7 minutes or until rice is tender and
vegetables are heated through.   *Makes 6 servings*

*For a spicy dish, use andouille sausage. Any type of kielbasa or
turkey kielbasa can also be used.

Glazed Cornish Hens

1 **package (7.2 ounces) RICE-A-RONI®
Herb & Butter**
1 **package (9 ounces) frozen cut green
beans**
¼ **teaspoon black pepper**
2 **cornish hens, split into halves** *or*
**1 broiler-fryer chicken (3 to
3½ pounds), quartered**
⅓ **cup apricot or peach preserves**
1 **tablespoon Dijon mustard**

1. Prepare Rice-A-Roni Mix as package directs. Add frozen green beans and pepper, stirring just until beans are separated.

2. Heat oven to 400°F. Spoon rice mixture into 11×7-inch glass baking dish; top with hen halves. Bake 30 minutes.

3. Combine preserves and mustard; brush hens with preserve mixture.

4. Continue baking 15 to 25 minutes or until hens are no longer pink inside and glaze is golden brown.

Makes 4 servings

Baked Potatoes with Tuna and Broccoli in Cheese Sauce

2 medium baking potatoes (6 to 8 ounces
    each)
1 package (10 ounces) frozen broccoli in
    cheese sauce
1 can (6 ounces) STARKIST® Solid
    White Tuna, drained and chunked
1 teaspoon chili powder
¼ cup minced green onions,
    including tops
2 slices cooked, crumbled bacon

Microwave Directions: Wash and pierce potatoes;
microwave on HIGH 8 minutes. Wrap in foil; let stand
to finish cooking while preparing broccoli. Microwave
vented pouch of broccoli on HIGH 5 minutes. In
medium microwavable bowl, combine tuna and chili
powder. Gently stir in broccoli. Cover; heat on HIGH
1½ more minutes or until heated through. Cut
potatoes in half lengthwise. Top with broccoli-tuna
mixture; sprinkle with onions and bacon.

Makes 2 servings

Poultry

PLUS

Hearty Chicken Bake

3 cups hot mashed potatoes
1 cup (4 ounces) shredded Cheddar
   cheese, divided
1⅓ cups (2.8 ounce can) FRENCH'S®
   French Fried Onions, divided
1½ cups (7 ounces) cubed cooked chicken
1 package (10 ounces) frozen mixed
   vegetables, thawed and drained
1 can (10¾ ounces) condensed cream of
   chicken soup
¼ cup milk
½ teaspoon ground mustard
¼ teaspoon garlic powder
¼ teaspoon pepper

Preheat oven to 375°F. In medium bowl, combine
mashed potatoes, *½ cup* cheese and *⅔ cup* French Fried
Onions; mix thoroughly. Spoon potato mixture into
greased 1½-quart casserole. Using back of spoon, spread
potatoes across bottom and up sides of dish to form a
shell. In large bowl, combine chicken, mixed
vegetables, soup, milk and seasonings; pour into potato
shell. Bake, uncovered, at 375°F for 30 minutes or
until heated through. Top with remaining *½ cup* cheese
and *⅔ cup* onions; bake, uncovered, 3 minutes or until
onions are golden brown. Let stand 5 minutes before
serving.   *Makes 4 to 6 servings*

Dairyland Confetti Chicken

1 cup diced carrots
¾ cup chopped onion
½ cup diced celery
¼ cup chicken broth
3 cups cubed cooked chicken
1 can (10¾ ounces) cream of chicken
    soup
1 cup sour cream
½ cup (4 ounces) sliced mushrooms
1 teaspoon Worcestershire sauce
1 teaspoon salt
⅛ teaspoon pepper
   Confetti Topping (recipe follows)
¼ cup (1 ounce) shredded Wisconsin
    Cheddar cheese

For casserole: In saucepan, combine carrots, onion, celery and chicken broth. Simmer 20 minutes. In 3-quart casserole, mix chicken cubes, soup, sour cream, mushrooms, Worcestershire sauce, salt and pepper. Add simmered vegetables and liquid; mix well. Prepare Confetti Topping. Drop tablespoons of topping onto casserole. Bake in preheated 350°F oven for 40 to 45 minutes or until golden brown. Sprinkle with cheese and return to oven until melted. Garnish as desired.   *Makes 6 to 8 servings*

Confetti Topping

1 **cup sifted all-purpose flour**
2 **teaspoons baking powder**
½ **teaspoon salt**
1 **cup (4 ounces) shredded Wisconsin**
   Cheddar cheese
2 **eggs, slightly beaten**
½ **cup milk**
1 **tablespoon chopped green bell pepper**
1 **tablespoon chopped pimiento**

In mixing bowl, combine flour, baking powder and salt. Add cheese, eggs, milk, green pepper and pimiento and mix just until well blended.

Favorite recipe from **Wisconsin Milk Marketing Board**

Chicken-Asparagus Casserole

2 teaspoons vegetable oil
1 cup chopped green and/or red bell
    peppers
1 medium onion, chopped
2 cloves garlic, minced
2 cups (8 ounces) shredded Cheddar
    cheese, divided
1 can (10¾ ounces) condensed cream of
    asparagus soup
1 container (8 ounces) ricotta cheese
2 eggs
1½ cups chopped cooked chicken, cut into
    ½-inch pieces
1 package (10 ounces) frozen chopped
    asparagus,* thawed and drained
8 ounces egg noodles, cooked
    Ground black pepper (optional)

1. Preheat oven to 350°F. Grease 13×9-inch casserole; set aside.

2. Heat oil in small skillet over medium heat. Add bell peppers, onion and garlic; cook and stir until crisp-tender.

3. Mix 1 cup Cheddar cheese, soup, ricotta cheese and eggs in large bowl until well blended. Add onion mixture, chicken, asparagus and noodles; mix well. Season with pepper, if desired.

4. Spread mixture evenly in prepared casserole. Top with remaining 1 cup Cheddar cheese.

5. Bake 30 minutes or until center is set and cheese is bubbly. Let stand 5 minutes before serving.

Makes 12 servings

*Or, substitute ½ pound fresh asparagus cut into ½-inch pieces. Bring 6 cups water to a boil over high heat in large saucepan. Add fresh asparagus. Reduce heat to medium. Cover and cook 5 to 8 minutes or until crisp-tender. Drain.

Almond-Chicken Casserole

>   1   cup fresh bread cubes
>   1   tablespoon margarine, melted
>   3   cups chopped cooked chicken
>   1½ cups celery slices
>   1   cup MIRACLE WHIP® Salad Dressing
>   1   cup (4 ounces) shredded 100% Natural
>   KRAFT® Swiss Cheese
>   ½   cup (1½-inch-long) red or green pepper
>   strips
>   ¼   cup slivered almonds, toasted
>   ¼   cup chopped onion

• Combine bread cubes and margarine; toss lightly. Set aside. Combine remaining ingredients; mix lightly. Spoon into 10×6-inch baking dish. Top with bread cubes. Bake at 350°F, 30 minutes or until lightly browned.

Makes 6 servings

Cheesy Chicken Roll-Ups

¼ cup butter
1 medium onion, diced
4 ounces fresh mushrooms, sliced
3 boneless skinless chicken breast halves,
    cut into bite-sized pieces
¾ cup dry white wine
½ teaspoon dried tarragon leaves, crushed
½ teaspoon salt
½ teaspoon pepper
6 lasagna noodles, cooked and drained
1 package (8 ounces) cream cheese,
    softened and cubed
½ cup heavy cream
½ cup sour cream
1½ cups (6 ounces) shredded Swiss
    cheese, divided
1 cup (4 ounces) shredded Muenster
    cheese, divided
3 tablespoons sliced almonds, toasted*
    Chopped parsley (optional)

1. Preheat oven to 325°F. Grease 13×9-inch baking pan; set aside.

2. Melt butter in large skillet over medium-high heat. Add onion and mushrooms; cook and stir until tender. Add chicken, wine, tarragon, salt and pepper; bring to a boil over high heat. Reduce heat to low. Simmer 10 minutes.

3. Cut lasagna noodles in half lengthwise. Curl each half into a circle; arrange in prepared pan. With slotted spoon, fill center of lasagna rings with chicken mixture, reserving liquid in skillet.

4. To remaining liquid in skillet, add cream cheese, heavy cream, sour cream, ¾ cup Swiss cheese and ½ cup Muenster cheese. Cook and stir over medium-low heat until cheese melts. *Do not boil.* Pour over lasagna rings. Sprinkle remaining cheeses and almonds on top.

5. Bake 35 minutes or until bubbly. Sprinkle with parsley.   *Makes 6 servings*

*To toast almonds, spread almonds in single layer on baking sheet. Bake in preheated 350°F oven 8 to 10 minutes or until golden brown, stirring frequently.

Apple Curry Chicken

- 4 boneless skinless chicken breasts
- 1 cup apple juice, divided
- ¼ teaspoon salt
  Dash of pepper
- 1 medium apple, cored and diced
- 1 medium onion, diced
- 1½ cups plain croutons
- ¼ cup raisins
- 2 teaspoons brown sugar
- 1 teaspoon curry powder
- ¾ teaspoon poultry seasoning
- ⅛ teaspoon garlic powder

Preheat oven to 350°F. Lightly grease 1-quart round baking dish. Arrange chicken breasts in single layer in prepared dish. Combine ¼ cup apple juice, salt and pepper in small bowl. Brush all of juice mixture over chicken.

Toss together apple and onion in large bowl. Stir in croutons, raisins, brown sugar, curry, poultry seasoning and garlic powder. Toss with remaining ¾ cup apple juice. Spread crouton mixture over chicken. Cover with foil or lid; bake 45 minutes or until chicken is tender. *Makes 4 servings*

"Wildly" Delicious Casserole

1 package (14 ounces) ground chicken
1 package (14 ounces) frozen broccoli
    with red peppers
1½ cups cooked wild rice
1 can (10¾ ounces) condensed cream of
    chicken soup
½ cup mayonnaise
½ cup plain yogurt
1 teaspoon lemon juice
½ teaspoon curry powder
¼ cup dry bread crumbs
3 to 4 slices process American cheese,
    cut in half diagonally

Preheat oven to 375°F. Grease 8-inch square baking dish; set aside. In large skillet, cook chicken until no longer pink, stirring occasionally. Drain; set aside. Cook broccoli and peppers according to package directions; set aside. In large bowl, combine wild rice, soup, mayonnaise, yogurt, lemon juice and curry. Stir in chicken and broccoli and peppers. Pour into prepared baking dish; sprinkle with bread crumbs. Bake 45 to 55 minutes or until heated through, arranging cheese slices on top of casserole during last 5 minutes of baking. Remove from oven; let stand 5 minutes. *Makes 6 to 8 servings*

Favorite recipe from **Minnesota Cultivated Wild Rice Council**

Mustard Chicken & Vegetables

- ¼ cup FRENCH'S® Dijon or CLASSIC YELLOW® Mustard
- ¼ cup vegetable oil
- 1 tablespoon red wine vinegar
- ½ teaspoon dried oregano, crumbled
- ¼ teaspoon pepper
- ¼ teaspoon salt
- 2 pounds chicken pieces, fat trimmed
- 2 cups (8 ounces) fusilli or rotini, cooked in unsalted water and drained
- 1 can (10¾ ounces) condensed cream of chicken soup
- ½ cup milk
- 1 cup each (1-inch) zucchini and yellow squash chunks
- 1⅓ cups (2.8 ounce can) FRENCH'S® French Fried Onions, divided
- 1 medium tomato, cut into wedges

Preheat oven to 375°F. In large bowl, combine mustard, oil, vinegar and seasonings; mix well. Toss chicken in mustard sauce until coated. Reserve remaining mustard sauce. Arrange chicken in 13×9-inch baking dish. Bake, uncovered, at 375°F for 30 minutes. Stir hot pasta, soup, milk, squash and ⅔ *cup* French Fried Onions into remaining mustard sauce. Spoon pasta mixture into baking dish, placing it under and around chicken. Bake, uncovered, 15 to 20 minutes or until chicken is done.

Top pasta mixture with tomato wedges and top chicken with remaining ⅔ *cup* onions. Bake, uncovered, 3 minutes or until onions are golden brown.

Makes 4 to 6 servings

Microwave Directions: Prepare mustard sauce as directed; add chicken and toss until coated. Reserve remaining mustard sauce. In 12×8-inch microwave-safe dish, arrange chicken with meatiest parts toward edges of dish. Cook, uncovered, on HIGH 10 minutes. Rearrange chicken. Prepare pasta mixture and add to chicken as above. Cook, uncovered, 15 to 17 minutes or until chicken and vegetables are done, stirring vegetables and pasta and rotating dish halfway through cooking time. Top with tomato wedges and remaining onions as directed; cook, uncovered, 1 minute. Let stand 5 minutes.

Fancy Chicken Puff Pie

4   tablespoons butter or margarine
¼   cup chopped shallots
¼   cup all-purpose flour
1   cup chicken broth or stock
¼   cup sherry
    Salt to taste
⅛   teaspoon white pepper
    Pinch ground nutmeg
¼   pound ham, cut into 2×¼-inch strips
3   cups cooked PERDUE® Chicken or
       OVEN STUFFER® Roaster, cut into
       2¼-inch strips
1½ cups coarsely chopped fresh asparagus
       or 1 (10-ounce) package frozen
       asparagus pieces
1   cup (½ pint) heavy cream
    Chilled pie crust for a 1-crust pie *or*
       1 sheet frozen puff pastry
1   egg, beaten

In medium saucepan, melt butter over medium-high heat. Add shallots; cook and stir until tender. Stir in flour; cook 3 minutes, stirring constantly. Add broth and sherry. Heat to boiling, stirring constantly; season with salt, pepper and nutmeg. Reduce heat to low; simmer 5 minutes, stirring occasionally. Stir in ham, chicken, asparagus and cream. Pour chicken mixture into ungreased 9-inch pie plate.

Preheat oven to 425°F. Cut 8-inch circle from crust. Place circle on cookie sheet moistened with cold water; pierce with fork. Brush with egg.

Bake crust and filled pie plate 10 minutes. Reduce heat to 350°F. Bake 10 to 15 minutes or until pastry is golden brown and filling is hot and set. With spatula, place pastry over hot filling.   *Makes 4 servings*

Easy Chicken Pot Pie

- 1¼ cups hot water
- 3 tablespoons margarine or butter, cut into pieces
- 3 cups STOVE TOP® Stuffing Mix for Chicken in the Canister
- 1 can (10¾ ounces) condensed cream of chicken soup
- 1 cup milk
- 3 cups cooked chicken or turkey cubes
- 1 package (10 ounces) frozen mixed vegetables, thawed
- 1 can (4 ounces) sliced mushrooms, drained
- ¼ teaspoon dried thyme leaves

HEAT oven to 350°F.

MIX hot water and margarine in large bowl until margarine is melted. Stir in stuffing mix just to moisten; set aside.

MIX soup and milk in another large bowl until smooth. Stir in chicken, vegetables, mushrooms and thyme. Pour into 12×8-inch glass baking dish. Spoon stuffing evenly over top.

BAKE 35 minutes or until heated through.
          Makes 4 to 6 servings

Chicken Biscuit Bake

BASE

- 1 tablespoon CRISCO® Vegetable Oil
- 1 cup chopped onion
- ¼ cup all-purpose flour
- ½ teaspoon salt
- ¼ teaspoon pepper
- ¼ teaspoon dried basil leaves
- ¼ teaspoon dried thyme leaves
- 2½ cups skim milk
- 1 tablespoon Worcestershire sauce
- 1 chicken flavor bouillon cube *or*
  1 teaspoon chicken flavor bouillon
  granules
- 2 cups chopped cooked chicken
- 1 bag (16 ounces) frozen mixed
  vegetables
- 2 tablespoons grated Parmesan cheese

BISCUITS

- 1 cup all-purpose flour
- 1 tablespoon sugar
- 1 tablespoon chopped fresh parsley
- 1½ teaspoons baking powder
- ⅛ teaspoon salt
- ⅓ cup skim milk
- 3 tablespoons CRISCO® Vegetable Oil

1. Heat oven to 375°F.

2. For base, heat Crisco® Oil in large saucepan over medium-high heat. Add onion. Cook and stir until tender. Remove from heat. Stir in flour, salt, pepper, basil and thyme. Add milk, Worcestershire sauce and bouillon cube. Return to medium-high heat. Cook and stir until mixture comes to a boil and is thickened. Stir in chicken, vegetables and cheese. Heat thoroughly, stirring occasionally. Pour into 2-quart casserole.

3. For biscuits, combine flour, sugar, parsley, baking powder and salt in medium bowl. Add milk and Crisco® Oil. Stir with fork until dry ingredients are just moistened.

4. Drop dough by well-rounded measuring tablespoonfuls onto hot chicken mixture to form 8 biscuits.

5. Bake at 375°F for 35 to 45 minutes or until chicken mixture is bubbly and biscuits are golden brown.

Makes 8 servings

Barbecue Chicken with Cornbread Topper

1½ pounds boneless skinless chicken
     breasts and thighs
1 can (15 ounces) red beans, rinsed and
     drained
1 can (8 ounces) tomato sauce
1 cup chopped green bell pepper
½ cup barbecue sauce
1 envelope (6.5 ounces) cornbread mix
     Ingredients for cornbread mix

1. Cut chicken into ¾-inch cubes. Heat nonstick skillet over medium heat. Add chicken; cook and stir 5 minutes or until cooked through.

2. Combine chicken, beans, tomato sauce, bell pepper and barbecue sauce in 8-inch microwavable ovenproof dish.

3. Preheat oven to 375°F. Loosely cover chicken mixture with plastic wrap or waxed paper. Microwave on MEDIUM-HIGH (70% power) 8 minutes or until heated through, stirring after 4 minutes.

4. While chicken mixture is heating, prepare cornbread mix according to package directions. Spoon batter over chicken mixture. Bake 15 to 18 minutes or until toothpick inserted in center of cornbread layer comes out clean.   *Makes 8 servings*

Curried Chicken Pot Pie

2 cups (10 ounces) cubed cooked chicken
1 bag (16 ounces) frozen vegetable
combination (cauliflower, carrots,
broccoli), thawed and drained
1⅓ cups (2.8 ounce can) FRENCH'S®
French Fried Onions, divided
1 cup (4 ounces) shredded Cheddar
cheese, divided
1 can (10¾ ounces) condensed cream of
chicken soup
⅔ cup milk
½ teaspoon seasoned salt
¼ teaspoon curry powder
1 (9-inch) folded refrigerated unbaked pie
crust

Preheat oven to 400°F. In 9-inch pie plate, combine
chicken, vegetables, ⅔ *cup* French Fried Onions and
½ *cup* cheese. In small bowl, combine soup, milk and
seasonings; pour over chicken mixture and stir to
combine. Place pie crust over chicken mixture; seal
edges and cut 4 steam vents. Bake, uncovered, at 400°F
for 40 minutes or until crust is golden brown. Top with
remaining ½ *cup* cheese and ⅔ *cup* onions; bake,
uncovered, 1 to 3 minutes or until onions are golden
brown.   *Makes 4 to 6 servings*

Broccoli Chicken Pasta Casserole

2   teaspoons CRISCO® Vegetable Oil
⅔   cup chopped onion
2   large cloves garlic, minced
1   pound boneless, skinless chicken
    breast, cut into 1-inch pieces
2   cans (14½ ounces each) whole
    tomatoes, undrained and chopped
1   can (8 ounces) tomato sauce
¼   cup ketchup
1¼ teaspoons dried basil leaves
¾   teaspoon dried oregano leaves
¼   teaspoon salt
1   package (10 ounces) frozen cut
    broccoli, thawed and well drained
5   ounces uncooked small macaroni,
    cooked and well drained
½   cup grated Parmesan cheese, divided

1. Heat oven to 350°F.

2. Heat Crisco® Oil in large skillet over medium-high heat. Add onion and garlic. Cook and stir until tender. Add chicken. Cook and stir until chicken is no longer pink. Stir in tomatoes, tomato sauce, ketchup, basil, oregano and salt. Bring to a boil. Reduce heat to low. Simmer 5 minutes, stirring occasionally.

3. Combine broccoli, macaroni, chicken mixture and ¼ cup cheese in large bowl. Stir well. Spoon into 13×9-inch baking dish. Sprinkle with remaining ¼ cup cheese. Bake at 350°F for 20 minutes.

Makes 8 servings

Chicken & Vegetable Lo Mein

1 can (13¾ ounces) reduced-sodium or
    regular chicken broth
1 cup coarsely chopped onion
1 package (4.7 ounces) PASTA RONI®
    Chicken & Broccoli with Linguine
1 package (16 ounces) frozen mixed
    cauliflower, carrots and snow peas
    vegetable medley
2 cups chopped cooked chicken or turkey
1 tablespoon reduced-sodium or regular
    soy sauce
2 teaspoons dark sesame oil (optional)

1. In 3-quart saucepan, combine 1 cup water, chicken broth and onion. Bring just to a boil.

2. Gradually add pasta while stirring. Separate pasta with a fork, if needed.

3. Stir in contents of seasoning packet. Reduce heat to medium.

4. Boil, uncovered, stirring frequently, 5 minutes. Stir in frozen vegetables and chicken. Boil over high heat, stirring frequently, 5 to 6 minutes or until pasta is desired tenderness, vegetables are tender and sauce is slightly thickened.

5. Stir in soy sauce. Stir in sesame oil.

Makes 4 servings

Italian Rotini Bake

- 8 ounces dried rotini pasta, cooked, drained and kept warm
- 1 tablespoon olive oil
- 1½ cups (2 small) sliced, quartered zucchini
- 1¼ cups (1 medium) chopped onion
- 2 cloves garlic, finely chopped
- 1 pound ground turkey
- 3½ cups (two 14.5-ounce cans) CONTADINA® Dalla Casa Buitoni Recipe Ready Diced Tomatoes, undrained
- ⅔ cup (6-ounce can) CONTADINA® Dalla Casa Buitoni Tomato Paste
- ½ cup water
- 1½ teaspoons Italian herb seasoning
- ½ teaspoon salt
- 1¾ cups (15-ounce container) ricotta cheese
- 3 cups (12 ounces) shredded mozzarella cheese, divided
- 1 egg

HEAT oil in large skillet over medium-high heat. Add zucchini, onion and garlic; cook 2 to 3 minutes or until vegetables are tender. Add turkey; cook 4 to 5 minutes or until turkey is no longer pink. Drain. Add tomatoes with juice, tomato paste, water, Italian herb seasoning and salt. Bring to a boil. Reduce heat to low; cook, stirring occasionally, for 5 to 6 minutes.

COMBINE ricotta cheese, *1 cup* mozzarella cheese and egg in medium bowl. Layer half of pasta, half of sauce, ricotta cheese mixture, *1 cup* mozzarella cheese, remaining pasta, remaining sauce and *remaining* mozzarella cheese in 13×9-inch baking dish.

BAKE, covered, in preheated 350°F. oven for 20 to 25 minutes or until heated through.

Makes 8 to 10 servings

Chicken Divan

⅔ **cup milk**
2 **tablespoons margarine or butter**
1 **package (4.8 ounces) PASTA RONI®**
   Corkscrew Pasta with Four Cheeses
2 **cups chopped cooked chicken or turkey**
2 **cups broccoli flowerets**
½ **cup croutons, coarsely crushed**

1. In round 3-quart microwaveable glass casserole, combine 1½ cups water, milk and margarine. Microwave, uncovered, on HIGH 4 to 5 minutes or until boiling.

2. Stir in pasta, contents of seasoning packet, chicken and broccoli.

3. Microwave, uncovered, on HIGH 12 to 13 minutes, stirring after 6 minutes.

4. Let stand 4 to 5 minutes or until desired consistency. Sauce will be thin, but will thicken upon standing. Stir before serving. Sprinkle with croutons.

Makes 4 servings

Rotini, Turkey and Mozzarella Casserole

- 8 ounces dried rotini pasta, cooked, drained
- 2 tablespoons olive or vegetable oil
- 1½ cups (2 small) thinly sliced zucchini
- 1 cup (1 small) chopped onion
- 2 cloves garlic, finely chopped
- 3½ cups (28-ounce can) CONTADINA® Dalla Casa Buitoni Crushed Tomatoes
- 2 cups cooked, cubed turkey, chicken, ham, smoked turkey or sausage
- ¾ cup whole kernel corn
- 2 teaspoons Italian herb seasoning, crushed
- ½ teaspoon salt
- ¼ teaspoon ground black pepper
- ¾ cup (3 ounces) grated Parmesan cheese
- 1½ cups (6 ounces) shredded mozzarella cheese
- 3 tablespoons chopped fresh parsley

HEAT oil in large skillet over medium-high heat. Add zucchini, onion and garlic; cook for 3 to 5 minutes or until vegetables are tender. Stir in tomatoes, turkey, corn, Italian herb seasoning, salt and pepper; cook for 2 minutes or until heated through. Remove from heat; stir in pasta.

LAYER half of pasta-tomato mixture in greased 13×9-inch baking dish. Sprinkle with half of Parmesan cheese and half of mozzarella cheese. Repeat layers.

BAKE in preheated 350°F. oven for 20 to 25 minutes or until heated through. Cool in dish for 5 minutes; sprinkle with parsley before serving.

Makes 8 servings

Chicken Paprikash

2 tablespoons margarine or butter
1 pound skinless, boneless chicken breasts or thighs, cut into 1-inch pieces
½ cup chopped onion
1 clove garlic, minced
1 tablespoon paprika
½ cup milk
1 package (4.7 ounces) PASTA RONI® Fettuccine Alfredo
1 green bell pepper, cut into strips
½ cup sour half-and-half or sour cream

1. In large skillet, melt margarine over medium heat. Add chicken, onion and garlic; cook 1 minute, stirring occasionally. Add paprika; continue cooking 2 minutes.

2. Add 1½ cups water, milk, pasta, contents of seasoning packet and green pepper. Bring just to a boil. Reduce heat to medium-low.

3. Boil, uncovered, stirring frequently, 9 to 11 minutes or until pasta is desired tenderness and chicken is no longer pink inside. (Sauce will thicken upon standing.) Stir in sour half-and-half before serving.

Makes 4 servings

Italian Antipasto Bake

2 cups rotini or elbow macaroni, cooked
   in unsalted water and drained
1 bag (16 ounces) frozen vegetable
   combination (broccoli, water
   chestnuts, red pepper), thawed and
   drained
2 chicken breast halves, skinned, boned
   and cut into strips
⅔ cup bottled Italian salad dressing
½ cup drained garbanzo beans (optional)
¼ cup sliced pitted ripe olives (optional)
¼ cup (1 ounce) grated Parmesan cheese
½ teaspoon Italian seasoning
1 cup (4 ounces) shredded mozzarella
   cheese, divided
1⅓ cups (2.8 ounce can) FRENCH'S®
   French Fried Onions, divided

Preheat oven to 350°F. In 13×9-inch baking dish,
combine hot pasta, vegetables, chicken, salad dressing,
garbanzo beans, olives, Parmesan cheese and Italian
seasoning. Stir in ½ *cup* mozzarella cheese and ½ *can*
French Fried Onions. Bake, covered, at 350°F for 35
minutes or until chicken is done. Top with remaining
½ *cup* mozzarella cheese and ⅔ *cup* onions; bake,
uncovered, 5 minutes or until onions are golden
brown.   *Makes 4 to 6 servings*

Microwave Directions: In 12×8-inch microwave-safe dish, combine ingredients, except chicken strips, as instructed. Arrange uncooked chicken strips around edges of dish. Cook, covered, on HIGH 6 minutes. Stir center of casserole; rearrange chicken and rotate dish. Cook, covered, 5 to 6 minutes or until chicken is done. Stir casserole to combine chicken and pasta mixture. Top with remaining mozzarella cheese and onions; cook, uncovered, 1 minute or until cheese melts. Let stand 5 minutes.

Chicken Fajitas Dijon

¼ cup GREY POUPON® Dijon Mustard
2 tablespoons vegetable oil, divided
2 tablespoons lime juice
1 clove garlic, minced
1 tablespoon chopped cilantro
1 teaspoon chili powder
½ teaspoon ground cumin
¼ to ½ teaspoon crushed red pepper flakes
1 pound boneless, skinless chicken
    breasts, cut into strips
2 small onions, sliced
1 medium red, yellow or green bell
    pepper, cut into strips
8 (8-inch) flour tortillas, warmed
    Sour cream, chopped tomatoes and
       shredded Cheddar cheese optional

In medium bowl, blend mustard, 1 tablespoon oil, lime juice, garlic, cilantro, chili powder, cumin and red pepper flakes. Add chicken, stirring to coat well. Refrigerate 1 hour.

In large skillet, over medium-high heat, sauté onions and bell pepper strips in remaining oil 2 to 3 minutes or until tender; remove from skillet. In same skillet, sauté chicken mixture 5 to 7 minutes or until done. Stir in onion mixture; heat through.

Serve chicken mixture in flour tortillas with sour cream, chopped tomatoes and cheese, if desired.

Makes 4 servings

Chicken Mexicana Casserole

2½ pounds boned chicken breasts, skinned
  and cut into 1-inch cubes
2 packages (1 ounce each) LAWRY'S®
  Taco Spices & Seasonings
2 cans (14½ ounces each) whole
  tomatoes, undrained and cut up
3 cups (12 ounces) shredded sharp
  Cheddar cheese, divided
1 can (7 ounces) diced green chiles,
  undrained
1 can (12 ounces) whole kernel corn,
  drained
1 package (8¼ ounces) corn muffin mix
2 eggs
¼ cup dairy sour cream

In large bowl, toss chicken cubes with Taco Spices &
Seasonings and tomatoes; blend well. Add 1 cup
cheese. Spread mixture evenly into 13×9-inch baking
dish. Spoon chiles over chicken mixture; sprinkle with
remaining cheese. Set aside. In medium bowl, combine
remaining ingredients; blend well. Drop by rounded
spoonfuls on top of casserole, spacing evenly. Bake in
350°F oven 50 to 60 minutes or until top is lightly
browned and sauce is bubbly. Remove from oven and
let stand about 20 minutes before serving.

Makes 10 to 12 servings

Chicken & Tortilla Casserole

¼ cup low sodium chicken broth, defatted
   and divided
½ cup finely chopped red bell pepper
½ cup finely chopped green bell pepper
½ cup finely chopped red onion
1 can (28 ounces) low sodium tomatoes,
   undrained
¼ cup GUILTLESS GOURMET® Spicy
   Nacho Dip
3 ounces (about 60) GUILTLESS
   GOURMET® Unsalted Baked Tortilla
   Chips, divided
1 cup cooked and shredded boneless
   chicken breast

NACHO SAUCE
   ¾ cup GUILTLESS GOURMET® Spicy
      Nacho Dip
   ¼ cup low fat sour cream
   ¼ cup skim milk

Preheat oven to 350°F. Heat 2 tablespoons broth in
medium nonstick skillet until hot. Add peppers and
onion; cook about 5 minutes, stirring often. Add
remaining 2 tablespoons broth and cook until peppers
are soft. Remove from heat; set aside. Drain off about
¾ juice from tomatoes; discard. Coarsely chop
tomatoes.

To assemble casserole, spread ¼ cup nacho dip on
bottom of 1½- to 2-quart casserole dish. Top with layer
of tortilla chips (about 30). Cover with pepper mixture,

followed by another layer of tortilla chips (about 30). Evenly spread chicken over chips; top with tomatoes and remaining juice. Combine Nacho Sauce ingredients in small saucepan; heat over medium heat 2 to 3 minutes or until warm. Drizzle half the mixture evenly over tomato layer.

Cover and bake about 25 to 35 minutes or until mixture bubbles. Drizzle casserole with remaining Nacho Sauce. *Makes 4 servings*

Green Enchiladas with Chicken

1 pound fresh tomatillos *or* 2 cans
(13 ounces each) tomatillos, drained
1 can (7 ounces) diced green chilies,
undrained
2 tablespoons vegetable oil
1 medium onion, finely chopped
1 clove garlic, minced
1 can (about 14 ounces) chicken broth
Vegetable oil for frying
12 (6-inch) corn tortillas
3 cups shredded cooked chicken
2½ cups (10 ounces) shredded Monterey
Jack cheese
1 cup sour cream
4 green onions with tops, thinly sliced
Cilantro sprigs for garnish

Preheat oven to 350°F. If using fresh tomatillos,
remove husks; wash thoroughly. Place tomatillos in
2-quart pan; add ½ inch water. Bring to a boil. Cover;
reduce heat and simmer 10 minutes or until tender.
Drain. Place tomatillos and chilies in blender or food
processor container fitted with metal blade; process
until puréed. Heat 2 tablespoons oil in large skillet
over medium heat. Add onion and garlic; cook until
onion is tender. Stir in purée and chicken broth.
Simmer, uncovered, until sauce has reduced to about
2½ cups and is consistency of canned tomato sauce.

Heat ½ inch oil in 7- to 8-inch skillet over medium-high heat. Place 1 tortilla in hot oil; cook 2 seconds on each side or just until limp. Drain briefly on paper towels, then dip softened tortilla into tomatillo sauce. Transfer sauced tortilla to a plate. Place about ¼ cup chicken and 2 tablespoons cheese across center of tortilla; roll to enclose. Place enchilada, seam side down, in 15×10-inch baking pan. Repeat until all tortillas are filled. Spoon remaining sauce over enchiladas, making sure all ends are moistened; reserve remaining cheese. Cover. Bake 20 to 30 minutes or until hot in center. Uncover and top with remaining cheese. Continue baking, uncovered, 10 minutes or until cheese is melted. Spoon sour cream down center of enchiladas; sprinkle with green onions. Garnish with cilantro.   *Makes 6 servings*

Chicken Enchiladas

1¾ cups fat free sour cream
½ cup chopped green onions
⅓ cup minced fresh cilantro
1 tablespoon minced fresh jalapeño chili pepper
1 teaspoon ground cumin
1 tablespoon vegetable oil
12 ounces boneless, skinless chicken breasts, cut into 3×1-inch strips
1 teaspoon minced garlic
8 flour tortillas (8-inch)
1 cup (4 ounces) shredded ALPINE LACE® Reduced Fat Cheddar Cheese
1 cup bottled chunky salsa (medium or hot)
1 small ripe tomato, chopped
Sprigs of cilantro (optional)

1. Preheat the oven to 350°F. Spray a 13×9×3-inch baking dish with nonstick cooking spray.

2. In a small bowl, mix together the sour cream, green onions, cilantro, jalapeño pepper and cumin.

3. Spray a large nonstick skillet with the cooking spray, pour in the oil and heat over medium-high heat. Add the chicken and garlic and sauté for 4 minutes or until the juices run clear when the chicken is pierced with a fork.

4. Divide the chicken strips among the 8 tortillas, placing them down the center of the tortillas. Top with the sour cream mixture, then roll them up and place them, seam side down, in the baking dish.

5. Sprinkle with the cheese, cover with foil and bake for 30 minutes or until bubbly. Spoon the salsa in a strip down the center and sprinkle the salsa with the tomato. Garnish with the sprigs of cilantro, if you wish. Serve hot!   *Makes 8 servings*

Chicken Fiesta

2½ to 3 pounds chicken pieces
   Salt
   Pepper
   Paprika
 2 tablespoons butter or margarine
 ¼ pound pork sausage
 ¾ cup sliced celery
 ¾ cup sliced green onions with tops
 3 cups cooked rice
 1 can (12 ounces) whole kernel corn with peppers, drained
 2 teaspoons lemon juice

Preheat oven to 350°F.

Season chicken with salt, pepper and paprika. In large skillet, melt butter. Add chicken to skillet; brown well. Drain chicken on paper towels; set aside. Cook sausage, celery and onions in same skillet over medium-high heat, stirring frequently, until vegetables are crisp-tender. Add rice, corn and lemon juice; mix well. Pour into prepared shallow baking dish. Arrange chicken on top of rice mixture, pressing chicken slightly into rice mixture. Cover with foil. Bake 30 to 40 minutes or until chicken is no longer pink in center.

Makes 6 servings

Favorite recipe from **USA Rice Council**

Tex-Mex Chicken & Rice Chili

1 package (6.8 ounces) RICE-A-RONI®
Spanish Rice
2 cups chopped cooked chicken or turkey
1 can (15 or 16 ounces) kidney beans or
pinto beans, rinsed and drained
1 can (14½ or 16 ounces) tomatoes or
stewed tomatoes, undrained
1 medium green bell pepper, cut into
½-inch pieces
1½ teaspoons chili powder
1 teaspoon ground cumin
½ cup (2 ounces) shredded Cheddar or
Monterey Jack cheese (optional)
Sour cream (optional)
Chopped cilantro (optional)

1. In 3-quart saucepan, combine rice-vermicelli mix, contents of seasoning packet, 2¾ cups water, chicken, beans, tomatoes, green pepper, chili powder and cumin. Bring to a boil over high heat.

2. Reduce heat to low; simmer, uncovered, about 20 minutes or until rice is tender, stirring occasionally.

3. Top with cheese, sour cream and cilantro, if desired.

Makes 4 servings

Chicken and Black Bean Chili

1 tablespoon vegetable oil
1 medium onion, chopped
4 boneless, skinless chicken breast halves
     (¾ to 1 pound), cooked and cut into
     strips
2 cans (14½ ounces each) diced
     tomatoes, undrained
1 can (15 ounces) black beans, rinsed
     and drained
1 can (4 ounces) diced green chiles,
     drained
½ cup water
½ teaspoon LAWRY'S® Garlic Powder with
     Parsley
1 package (1.48 ounces) LAWRY'S®
     Spices & Seasonings for Chili
½ teaspoon hot pepper sauce (optional)
1 tablespoon chopped fresh cilantro

In large, deep skillet, heat oil. Add onion; sauté until
tender and translucent. Add all remaining ingredients
except cilantro. Bring to a boil. Reduce heat to low;
simmer, uncovered, 20 minutes, stirring occasionally.
Stir in cilantro.   *Makes 5½ cups*

Variation: Substitute 1½ pounds ground turkey or
chicken, browned in 1 tablespoon oil, for shredded
chicken.

20-Minute White Bean Chili

1 **cup chopped onions**
1 **clove garlic, minced**
1 **tablespoon vegetable oil**
1 **pound ground turkey**
1 **cup COLLEGE INN® Chicken Broth or Lower Sodium Chicken Broth**
1 **(14½-ounce) can stewed tomatoes**
⅓ **cup GREY POUPON® Dijon Mustard**
1 **tablespoon chili powder**
⅛ **to ¼ teaspoon ground red pepper**
1 **(15-ounce) can cannellini beans, drained and rinsed**
1 **(8-ounce) can corn, drained**
  Tortilla chips, shredded Cheddar cheese and cilantro, optional

In 3-quart saucepan, over medium-high heat, sauté onions and garlic in oil until tender. Add turkey; cook until done, stirring occasionally to break up meat. Drain. Stir in chicken broth, tomatoes, mustard, chili powder and pepper. Heat to a boil; reduce heat. Simmer for 10 minutes. Stir in beans and corn; cook for 5 minutes. Top with tortilla chips, shredded cheese and cilantro, if desired. *Makes 6 servings*

Arizona Turkey Stew

5   medium carrots, cut into thick slices
1   large onion, cut into ½-inch pieces
3   tablespoons olive oil or vegetable oil
1   pound sliced turkey breast, cut into
       1-inch strips
1   teaspoon LAWRY'S® Garlic Powder with
       Parsley
3   tablespoons all-purpose flour
8   small red potatoes, cut into ½-inch
       cubes
1   package (10 ounces) frozen peas,
       thawed
8   ounces sliced fresh mushrooms
1   cup beef broth
1   can (8 ounces) tomato sauce
1   package (1.48 ounces) LAWRY'S®
       Spices & Seasonings for Chili

Preheat oven to 450°F. In large skillet over medium
heat, cook and stir carrots and onion in oil until
tender. Stir in turkey strips and Garlic Powder with
Parsley; cook 3 minutes or until turkey is just
browned. Stir in flour. Pour mixture into 3-quart
casserole dish. Stir in remaining ingredients. Bake,
covered, 40 to 45 minutes or until potatoes are tender
and turkey is no longer pink in center. Let stand
5 minutes before serving.   *Makes 8 to 10 servings*

Stovetop Directions: Prepare recipe as directed, substituting Dutch oven for skillet and casserole dish. Bring mixture to a boil. Reduce heat; cover and simmer 40 to 45 minutes or until potatoes are tender and turkey is no longer pink in center. Let stand 5 minutes before serving.

Hint: Spoon dollops of prepared dumpling mix on top of casserole during last 15 minutes of baking.

He-Man Stew

1   **package (about 3½ pounds) PERDUE®
     Fresh Skinless Pick of the Chicken
     Salt and ground pepper**
2   **tablespoons olive oil**
1   **can (28 ounces) whole plum tomatoes,
     drained and chopped**
1   **can (12 ounces) lite beer**
1   **onion, sliced into rings**
¼   **cup spicy brown mustard**
4   **cups cooked elbow macaroni (optional)**

Season chicken with salt and pepper to taste. In large nonstick skillet over medium-high heat, heat oil. Add chicken; cook 5 to 6 minutes on each side for larger pieces, 3 to 4 minutes on each side for smaller pieces, or until brown, turning often. In large slow cooker, combine tomatoes, beer, onion and mustard. Add chicken. Cook on high 1½ to 2 hours, or until chicken is fork-tender. Serve over macaroni.

Makes 3 to 4 servings

Southwestern Pumpkin Stew

1   tablespoon vegetable oil
1   pound boneless, skinless chicken breast
      meat, cut into 1-inch pieces
1   cup (1 small) chopped onion
½   cup (1 large) sliced carrot
1   cup (2 large stalks) sliced celery
½   cup chopped red bell pepper
1¾ cups (15-ounce can) LIBBY'S® Solid
      Pack Pumpkin
1¾ cups (14.5-ounce can) chicken broth
1¼ cups (15-ounce can) hominy
½   cup sour cream
3   tablespoons chopped fresh cilantro
½   teaspoon salt
½   teaspoon ground black pepper
½   teaspoon dried oregano, crushed
½   teaspoon ground cumin
⅛   teaspoon ground nutmeg

HEAT oil in large saucepan over medium-high heat.
Add chicken, onion and carrot; cook for 3 to 4 minutes
or until chicken is no longer pink. Add celery and bell
pepper; cook for 3 to 4 minutes or until vegetables are
crisp-tender.

STIR in pumpkin, broth, hominy, sour cream,
cilantro, salt, pepper, oregano, cumin and nutmeg.
Reduce heat to low; cook, stirring occasionally, for
10 to 15 minutes or until flavors are blended.

Makes 6 to 8 servings

Catalonian Stew

2 boneless skinless chicken breasts, cut
   into bite-size pieces
3 ounces pepperoni, diced
1 tablespoon vegetable oil
2 cans (15 ounces each) tomato sauce
3 cups chicken broth
1 cup pimiento-stuffed olives, halved
2 tablespoons sugar
8 ounces uncooked rotini or other shaped
   pasta
⅓ cup chopped parsley
⅛ teaspoon crushed saffron (optional)
1 cup (4 ounces) SARGENTO® Fancy
   Shredded Mild or Sharp Cheddar
   Cheese
1 cup (4 ounces) SARGENTO® Fancy
   Shredded Monterey Jack Cheese

In Dutch oven, cook chicken and pepperoni in oil over
medium heat until chicken is lightly browned, about
5 minutes; drain. Add tomato sauce, chicken broth,
olives and sugar. Bring to a boil; reduce heat and
simmer, covered, 15 minutes. Return to a boil. Add
rotini, parsley and saffron, if desired; cover and cook an
additional 15 minutes or until pasta is tender. Combine
Cheddar and Monterey Jack cheeses in small bowl.
Spoon stew into 6 individual ovenproof serving bowls;
sprinkle evenly with cheese. Bake in preheated 350°F
oven about 5 minutes until cheese is melted.

Makes 6 servings

Quick and Easy Sausage Stew

1 package (12 ounces) HEBREW
    NATIONAL® Lean Smoked Turkey
    Sausage or Beef Polish Sausage, cut
    into 1-inch slices
1 large onion, chopped
2 cloves garlic, minced
1 red bell pepper, seeded, cut into
    1-inch pieces
1 green bell pepper, seeded, cut into
    1-inch pieces
1 medium zucchini, cut into ½-inch slices
8 ounces fresh mushrooms, thickly sliced
2 cans (14½ ounces each) stewed
    tomatoes, undrained
1 teaspoon dried basil leaves
¼ teaspoon crushed red pepper
¼ teaspoon salt

Cook sausage, onion and garlic in large deep nonstick skillet over medium-high heat 3 minutes. Add bell peppers, zucchini and mushrooms; cook 5 minutes, stirring occasionally.

Add stewed tomatoes with liquid, basil, crushed pepper and salt. Bring to a boil. Reduce heat. Cover; simmer 25 minutes, stirring occasionally.

Makes 6 servings

Paella à la Española

2 tablespoons margarine or butter
1¼ to 1½ pounds chicken thighs, skinned
1 package (7.2 ounces) RICE-A-RONI®
   Rice Pilaf
1 can (14½ or 16 ounces) tomatoes or
   stewed tomatoes, undrained
½ teaspoon turmeric (optional)
⅛ teaspoon hot pepper sauce or black
   pepper
8 ounces cooked deveined, shelled
   medium shrimp
1 cup frozen peas
   Lemon wedges

1. In large skillet, melt margarine over medium heat. Add chicken; cook 2 minutes on each side or until browned. Remove from skillet; set aside, reserving drippings. Keep warm.

2. In same skillet, sauté rice-pasta mix in reserved drippings over medium heat until rice is lightly browned. Stir in 1½ cups water, tomatoes, turmeric, hot pepper sauce and contents of seasoning packet. Bring to a boil over high heat; stir in chicken.

3. Cover; reduce heat. Simmer 20 minutes. Stir in shrimp and frozen peas.

4. Cover; continue to simmer 5 to 10 minutes or until liquid is absorbed and rice is tender. Serve with lemon wedges.   *Makes 4 servings*

Orange Ginger Chicken & Rice

1 **package (6.9 ounces) RICE-A-RONI®
    With ⅓ Less Salt Chicken Flavor**
1 **tablespoon margarine or butter**
1 **cup orange juice**
¾ **pound skinless, boneless chicken
    breasts, cut into thin strips**
2 **cloves garlic, minced**
¼ **teaspoon ground ginger
    Dash crushed red pepper flakes
    (optional)**
3 **cups broccoli flowerets *or* 1½ cups
    short, thin carrot strips**

1. In large skillet, sauté rice-vermicelli mix and margarine over medium heat, stirring frequently, until vermicelli is golden brown.

2. Stir in 1½ cups water, orange juice, chicken, garlic, ginger, red pepper flakes and contents of seasoning packet; bring to a boil over high heat.

3. Cover; reduce heat. Simmer 10 minutes.

4. Stir in broccoli.

5. Cover; continue to simmer 5 to 10 minutes or until liquid is absorbed and rice is tender.

Makes 4 servings

Lemon-Garlic Chicken & Rice

4 skinless, boneless chicken breast halves
1 teaspoon paprika
  Salt and pepper (optional)
2 tablespoons margarine or butter
2 cloves garlic, minced
1 package (6.9 ounces) RICE-A-RONI®
  Chicken Flavor
2 tablespoons lemon juice
1 cup chopped red or green bell pepper
½ teaspoon grated lemon peel

1. Sprinkle chicken with paprika, salt and pepper.

2. In large skillet, melt margarine over medium-high heat. Add chicken and garlic; cook chicken 2 minutes on each side or until browned. Remove chicken from skillet; set aside, reserving drippings. Keep warm.

3. In same skillet, sauté rice-vermicelli mix in reserved drippings over medium heat until vermicelli is golden brown. Stir in 2¼ cups water, lemon juice and contents of seasoning packet. Top rice with chicken; bring to a boil over high heat.

4. Cover; reduce heat. Simmer 10 minutes. Stir in bell pepper and lemon peel.

5. Cover; continue to simmer 10 minutes or until liquid is absorbed, rice is tender and chicken is no longer pink inside.   *Makes 4 servings*

Chicken and Vegetable Risotto

Nonstick olive oil cooking spray
2   cups sliced mushrooms
½   cup chopped onion (about 1 small)
4   cloves garlic, minced
¼   cup finely chopped fresh parsley *or*
      1 tablespoon dried parsley leaves
3   to 4 tablespoons finely chopped fresh
      basil *or* 1 tablespoon dried basil
      leaves
6   cups defatted low-sodium chicken broth
1½ cups uncooked arborio rice or converted
      rice
2   cups broccoli florets, cooked crisp-
      tender
1   pound chicken tenders, cut into
      1½-inch pieces and cooked
4   plum tomatoes, seeded and chopped
½   teaspoon salt
½   teaspoon pepper
2   tablespoons grated Parmesan or
      Romano cheese

1. Spray large nonstick saucepan with cooking spray; heat over medium heat until hot. Add mushrooms, onion and garlic; cook and stir about 5 minutes or until tender. Add parsley and basil; cook and stir 1 minute.

2. Heat chicken broth to a boil in medium saucepan. Reduce heat to low; simmer.

3. Add rice to mushroom mixture; cook and stir over medium heat 1 to 2 minutes. Add chicken broth to mushroom mixture, ½ cup at a time, stirring constantly until broth is absorbed before adding next ½ cup. Continue adding broth and stirring until rice is tender and mixture is creamy, 20 to 25 minutes.

4. Add broccoli, chicken, tomatoes, salt and pepper. Cook and stir 2 to 3 minutes or until heated through. Sprinkle with cheese.   *Makes 4 servings*

Chicken Fried Rice

½ **cup sliced green onions**
¼ **cup sliced celery**
¼ **cup chopped red bell pepper**
1 **clove garlic, crushed**
½ **teaspoon grated gingerroot**
¼ **teaspoon crushed red pepper flakes**
2 **teaspoons peanut oil**
6 **tablespoons EGG BEATERS® Healthy Real Egg Product**
3 **cups cooked regular long-grain rice**
2 **cups diced cooked chicken**
2 **tablespoons reduced-sodium soy sauce**
1 **teaspoon sugar**

In large nonstick skillet, over high heat, sauté green onions, celery, bell pepper, garlic, ginger and crushed red pepper in oil until tender-crisp. Pour Egg Beaters® into skillet; cook, stirring occasionally until mixture is set. Stir in rice, chicken, soy sauce and sugar; cook until heated through.   *Makes 6 servings*

Peanut Chicken Stir-Fry

1   package (6.1 ounces) RICE-A-RONI®
    With ⅓ Less Salt Fried Rice
½   cup reduced-sodium or regular chicken
    broth
2   tablespoons creamy peanut butter
1   tablespoon reduced-sodium or regular
    soy sauce
1   tablespoon vegetable oil
¾   pound skinless, boneless chicken
    breasts, cut into ½-inch pieces
2   cloves garlic, minced
2   cups frozen mixed carrots, broccoli and
    red pepper vegetable medley, thawed
    and drained
2   tablespoons chopped peanuts (optional)

1. Prepare Rice-A-Roni Mix as package directs.

2. While Rice-A-Roni is simmering, combine chicken broth, peanut butter and soy sauce; mix with a fork. Set aside.

3. In second large skillet or wok, heat oil over medium high heat. Stir-fry chicken and garlic 2 minutes.

4. Add vegetables and broth mixture; stir-fry 5 to 7 minutes or until sauce has thickened. Serve over rice. Sprinkle with peanuts, if desired.

Makes 4 servings

Chicken Gumbo

2 tablespoons vegetable oil
¾ pound skinless, boneless chicken
    breasts or thighs, cut into ½-inch
    pieces
½ cup chopped onion
⅓ cup sliced celery
2 cloves garlic, minced
1 can (14½ ounces) tomatoes, undrained
    and coarsely chopped
1 can (13¾ ounces) reduced-sodium or
    regular chicken broth
½ cup chopped green bell pepper
½ teaspoon dried thyme leaves
⅛ teaspoon hot pepper sauce (optional)
1 bay leaf (optional)
1 package (6.8 ounces) RICE-A-RONI®
    Spanish Rice

1. In 3-quart saucepan, heat oil over medium heat. Add chicken, onion, celery and garlic; cook 3 to 4 minutes or until chicken is no longer pink.

2. Add ¾ cup water, tomatoes, chicken broth, bell pepper, thyme, hot pepper sauce, bay leaf, rice-vermicelli mix and contents of seasoning packet. Bring to a boil over high heat; reduce heat. Simmer 15 to 20 minutes or until rice is tender, stirring occasionally.

Makes 4 servings

Chicken Bourguignonne

4 **pounds skinless chicken thighs and
breasts**
Flour
Nonstick cooking spray
2 **cups defatted low-sodium chicken broth**
2 **cups dry white wine or defatted
low-sodium chicken broth**
1 **pound whole baby carrots**
¼ **cup tomato paste**
4 **cloves garlic, minced**
½ **teaspoon dried thyme leaves**
2 **bay leaves**
¼ **teaspoon salt**
¼ **teaspoon pepper**
8 **ounces fresh or thawed frozen
pearl onions**
8 **ounces whole medium mushrooms**
2 **cups hot cooked white rice**
2 **cups hot cooked wild rice**
¼ **cup minced fresh parsley**

1. Preheat oven to 325°F. Coat chicken very lightly
with flour. Generously spray nonstick ovenproof Dutch
oven or large nonstick ovenproof skillet with cooking
spray; heat over medium heat until hot. Cook chicken
10 to 15 minutes or until browned on all sides. Drain
fat from Dutch oven.

2. Add chicken broth, wine, carrots, tomato paste,
garlic, thyme, bay leaves, salt and pepper to Dutch
oven; heat to a boil. Cover; transfer to oven. Bake

1 hour. Add onions and mushrooms. Uncover; bake about 35 minutes or until vegetables are tender and chicken is no longer pink in center and juices run clear. Remove bay leaves. Combine white and wild rice; serve with chicken. Sprinkle rice with parsley.

Makes 8 servings

Polynesian Chicken and Rice

1   can (20 ounces) DOLE® Pineapple
     Tidbits or Pineapple Chunks
½   cup DOLE® Seedless or Golden Raisins
½   cup sliced DOLE® Green Onions
2   teaspoons finely chopped fresh ginger
     or ½ teaspoon ground ginger
1   clove garlic, finely chopped
3   cups cooked white or brown rice
2   cups chopped cooked chicken breast or
     turkey breast
2   tablespoons low-sodium soy sauce

• **Drain** pineapple; reserve 4 tablespoons juice.

• **Heat** 2 tablespoons reserved juice over medium heat in large, nonstick skillet. Add raisins, green onions, ginger and garlic; cook and stir 3 minutes.

• **Stir** in pineapple, rice, chicken, soy sauce and remaining 2 tablespoons juice. Cover; reduce heat to low and cook 5 minutes more or until heated through.

Makes 4 servings

Creamy Turkey & Broccoli

1 package (6 ounces) stuffing mix, plus
   ingredients to prepare mix*
1⅓ cups (2.8 ounce can) FRENCH'S®
   French Fried Onions, divided
1 package (10 ounces) frozen broccoli
   spears, thawed and drained
1 package (about 1⅛ ounces) cheese
   sauce mix
1¼ cups milk
½ cup sour cream
2 cups (10 ounces) cubed cooked turkey
   or chicken

Preheat oven to 350°F. In medium saucepan, prepare
stuffing mix according to package directions; stir in
⅔ cup French Fried Onions. Spread stuffing over
bottom of greased 9-inch round baking dish. Arrange
broccoli spears over stuffing with flowerets around
edge of dish. In medium saucepan, prepare cheese
sauce mix according to package directions using
1¼ cups milk. Remove from heat; stir in sour cream
and turkey. Pour turkey mixture over broccoli,
covering stalks only. Bake, covered, at 350°F for 30
minutes or until heated through. Sprinkle remaining
⅔ cup onions over turkey; bake, uncovered, 5 minutes
or until onions are golden brown.

Makes 4 to 6 servings

*3 cups leftover stuffing may be substituted for stuffing mix. If
stuffing is dry, stir in water, 1 tablespoon at a time, until moist but
not wet.

Microwave Directions: In 9-inch round microwave-safe dish, prepare stuffing mix according to package microwave directions; stir in ⅔ *cup* onions. Arrange stuffing and broccoli spears in dish as directed; set aside. In medium microwave-safe bowl, prepare cheese sauce mix according to package microwave directions using 1¼ cups milk. Add turkey and cook, covered, 5 to 6 minutes, stirring turkey halfway through cooking time. Stir in sour cream. Pour turkey mixture over broccoli, covering stalks only. Cook, covered, 8 to 10 minutes or until heated through, rotating dish halfway through cooking time. Top turkey with remaining ⅔ *cup* onions; cook, uncovered, 1 minute. Let stand 5 minutes.

Turkey Wild Rice Supreme

2 pounds ground turkey
½ cup butter
1 can (8 ounces) mushrooms, drained
1 cup chopped onions
½ cup chopped celery
½ cup shredded carrots
2 cups sour cream
¼ cup soy sauce
1 teaspoon salt
¼ teaspoon pepper
6 cups cooked wild rice (1½ cups
    uncooked)
½ cup slivered almonds

Preheat oven to 350°F. Grease 3-quart casserole. Set aside.

Cook turkey in large skillet over medium heat, stirring occasionally. Remove turkey from skillet and set aside. Melt butter in same skillet. Add mushrooms, onions, celery and carrots; cook and stir 5 to 10 minutes or until crisp-tender. Combine sour cream, soy sauce, salt and pepper. Add wild rice, turkey, mushroom mixture and almonds. Toss lightly. Place mixture in prepared casserole. Bake 45 minutes or until lightly browned, stirring several times during baking. Season with salt and pepper to taste. *Makes 10 to 12 servings*

Favorite recipe from **Minnesota Cultivated Wild Rice Council**

Homespun Turkey 'n' Vegetables

1　can (14 ounces) sliced carrots, drained
1　package (9 ounces) frozen cut green
　　beans, thawed and drained
1⅓　cups (2.8 ounce can) FRENCH'S®
　　French Fried Onions, divided
1　can (16 ounces) whole potatoes,
　　drained
1　can (10¾ ounces) condensed cream of
　　celery soup
¼　cup milk
1　tablespoon FRENCH'S® CLASSIC
　　YELLOW® Mustard
¼　teaspoon garlic powder
1　pound uncooked turkey breast slices

Preheat oven to 375°F. In 12×8-inch baking dish,
combine carrots, green beans and ⅔ cup French Fried
Onions. Slice potatoes in half; arrange as many halves
as will fit, cut-side down, around edges of baking dish.
Combine any remaining potatoes with vegetables in
dish. In medium bowl, combine soup, milk, mustard
and garlic powder; pour half of soup mixture over
vegetables. Overlap turkey slices on vegetables. Pour
remaining soup mixture over turkey and potatoes.
Bake, covered, at 375°F for 40 minutes or until turkey
is done. Top turkey with remaining ⅔ cup onions; bake,
uncovered, 3 minutes or until onions are golden.

Makes 4 servings

Turkey-Olive Ragoût en Croûte

½ pound boneless white or dark turkey
    meat, cut into 1-inch cubes
1 clove garlic, minced
1 teaspoon vegetable oil
¼ cup (about 10) small whole frozen
    onions
1 medium unpeeled red potato, cut into
    ½-inch cubes
½ cup reduced-sodium chicken or turkey
    broth
½ teaspoon dried parsley flakes, crumbled
⅛ teaspoon dried thyme leaves, crumbled
1 small bay leaf
10 frozen snow peas
8 whole small pitted ripe olives
1 can (4 ounces) refrigerated crescent
    rolls
½ teaspoon dried dill weed, crumbled

1. Preheat oven to 375°F.

2. In medium skillet over medium heat, cook and stir turkey and garlic in oil 3 to 4 minutes or until no longer pink; remove and set aside. Add onions to skillet; cook and stir until lightly browned. Add potato, broth, parsley, thyme and bay leaf. Bring mixture to a boil. Reduce heat; cover and simmer 10 minutes or until potato is tender. Remove and discard bay leaf.

3. Combine turkey mixture with potato mixture. Stir in snow peas and olives. Divide mixture between 2 (1¾-cup) individual ovenproof casseroles.

4. Divide crescent rolls into 2 rectangles; press perforations together to seal. If necessary, roll out each rectangle to make dough large enough to cover top of each casserole. Sprinkle dough with dill weed; press lightly into dough.

5. Cut small decorative shape from each dough piece; discard cutouts or place on baking sheet and bake in oven with casseroles. Place dough over turkey-vegetable mixture in casseroles. Trim dough to fit; press dough to edge of each casserole to seal. Bake 7 to 8 minutes or until pastry is golden brown.

Makes 2 individual deep-dish pies

Lattice-Crust Variation: With pastry wheel or knife, cut each rectangle lengthwise into 6 strips. Arrange strips, lattice-fashion, over turkey-vegetable mixture; trim dough to fit. Press ends of dough to edge of each casserole to seal.

Note: For a more golden crust, brush top of dough with beaten egg yolk before baking.

Favorite recipe from **National Turkey Federation**

Tasty Turkey Pot Pie

½ cup MIRACLE WHIP® Salad Dressing
2 tablespoons all-purpose flour
1 teaspoon instant chicken bouillon
⅛ teaspoon pepper
¾ cup milk
1½ cups chopped cooked turkey or chicken
1 (10-ounce) package frozen mixed
   vegetables, thawed and drained
1 (4-ounce) can refrigerated crescent
   rolls

• Combine salad dressing, flour, bouillon and pepper in medium saucepan. Gradually add milk.

• Cook, stirring constantly, over low heat until thickened. Add turkey and vegetables; heat thoroughly, stirring occasionally.

• Spoon into 8-inch square baking dish. Unroll dough into two rectangles. Press perforations together to seal. Place rectangles side-by-side to form square; press edges together to form seam. Cover turkey mixture with dough.

• Bake at 375°F 15 to 20 minutes or until browned.

Makes 4 to 6 servings

Colorful Turkey Pasta Bake

2 cups (about 8 ounces) uncooked mixed
   vegetable rotini pasta*
1 tablespoon margarine
1 tablespoon all-purpose flour
¼ teaspoon salt
⅛ teaspoon pepper
1⅓ cups skim milk
1 cup (4 ounces) shredded Swiss cheese,
   divided
2 cups cubed cooked turkey

1. Cook pasta according to package directions; drain.
In 2-quart saucepan, melt margarine over medium
heat. Stir in flour, salt and pepper. Blend in milk; cook,
stirring constantly, until thickened and bubbly. Add
¾ cup cheese; stir until melted. Stir in turkey and
pasta.

2. Spray 8-inch square baking dish with nonstick
vegetable spray. Add pasta mixture; sprinkle with
remaining ¼ cup cheese. Bake at 350°F until heated
through, about 30 minutes. Cut into squares to serve.

Makes 4 servings

*If desired, substitute elbow macaroni, rotelle, small shells or ziti for
rotini.

Favorite recipe from **National Turkey Federation**

Summer Turkey Lasagna

3   zucchini squash (8 to 9 inches long),
       sliced lengthwise into ¼-inch strips
½   pound turkey ham, cut into ½-inch
       cubes
1   can (8 ounces) no-salt tomato sauce
1   cup instant rice
½   medium onion, finely chopped
½   teaspoon Italian seasoning
⅛   teaspoon pepper
1   cup low-fat cottage cheese
½   cup (2 ounces) low-fat mozzarella
       cheese
1   teaspoon parsley flakes
2   tablespoons grated Parmesan cheese

1. In 8-inch square microwave-safe dish, layer zucchini
strips; cover with waxed paper. Microwave on HIGH
(100%) 8 to 10 minutes or until zucchini are tender,
rotating dish after 5 minutes. Remove zucchini; place
on paper towels to drain. Drain liquid from dish.

2. In medium bowl, combine turkey, tomato sauce,
rice, onion, Italian seasoning and pepper. Combine
cottage cheese, mozzarella cheese and parsley in small
bowl.

3. Arrange ½ of zucchini strips in single layer on
bottom of same microwave-safe dish. Top with turkey-
rice mixture, spreading to cover zucchini layer. Top
with cheese mixture; spread gently to cover turkey
mixture. Top with layer of remaining zucchini strips;
sprinkle with Parmesan cheese.

4. Microwave at MEDIUM (50%) 20 to 25 minutes or until rice is tender.   *Makes 4 servings*

Favorite recipe from **National Turkey Federation**

Curried Turkey and Couscous Skillet

- 1   tablespoon vegetable or olive oil
- 1   small onion, chopped
- 2   cloves garlic, minced
- 1   can (10½ ounces) kosher condensed chicken broth
- ⅓   cup water
- 2   teaspoons curry powder
- ¼   teaspoon ground red pepper
- 2   cups small broccoli flowerets
- 1   cup thinly sliced carrots
- 2   packages (4 ounces each) HEBREW NATIONAL® Sliced Oven Roasted Turkey Breast, cut into ½-inch strips
- 1   cup uncooked couscous
     Chopped fresh cilantro for garnish

Heat oil in large deep nonstick skillet over medium heat. Add onion and garlic; cook 5 minutes or until onion is tender. Add broth, water, curry powder and ground red pepper to skillet; bring to a boil. Stir in broccoli and carrots. Cover; simmer 5 minutes or until vegetables are crisp-tender. Stir turkey into broth mixture; cook until heated through. Stir in couscous, mixing well. Cover; remove from heat. Let stand 5 minutes or until liquid is absorbed. Garnish with cilantro, if desired.   *Makes 4 servings*

Dilled Turkey Noodle Bake

1 cup chopped celery
½ cup chopped onion
⅓ cup chopped green bell pepper
1 tablespoon margarine
2 tablespoons all-purpose flour
1¾ cups skim milk
2 teaspoons dried parsley flakes
1 teaspoon dried dill weed
¾ teaspoon salt
½ teaspoon pepper
4 cups egg noodles, cooked according to
   package directions and drained
2 cups (½-inch) cubed cooked turkey
1 cup non-fat sour cream
¼ cup seasoned dry bread crumbs

1. In large nonstick skillet over medium heat, sauté celery, onion and green pepper in margarine 5 minutes or until vegetables are tender. Reduce heat to low; stir in flour. Cook 1 minute, stirring constantly. Gradually add milk, stirring constantly. Stir in parsley, dill, salt and pepper; cook 1 to 2 minutes or until sauce is thickened. Remove from heat.

2. Add noodles, turkey and sour cream to skillet; mix well. Spray 11×7-inch baking dish with nonstick cooking spray. Add noodle mixture; sprinkle with bread crumbs. Bake at 350°F 30 minutes or until hot and bubbly.   *Makes 4 servings*

Favorite recipe from **National Turkey Federation**

Creamy Creole Turkey Bake

- ⅔ cup chopped onion
- ⅔ cup chopped celery
- ⅓ cup chopped green bell pepper
- 1 clove garlic, minced
- 1 tablespoon margarine
- ¼ pound mushrooms, sliced
- 4 ounces reduced-fat cream cheese, softened
- 1 can (8 ounces) low-sodium stewed tomatoes, drained
- 1½ teaspoons creole seasoning
- 4 ounces fettuccini, cooked according to package directions and drained
- 2 cups cubed cooked turkey (½-inch) Nonstick cooking spray
- ¼ cup grated Parmesan cheese

1. In medium nonstick skillet over medium-high heat, sauté onion, celery, green pepper and garlic in margarine 4 to 5 minutes or until vegetables are crisp-tender. Add mushrooms; sauté 2 minutes. Remove from heat.

2. In medium bowl, blend cream cheese, tomatoes and creole seasoning. Stir in vegetable mixture, fettuccini and turkey.

3. Pour mixture into 9-inch square baking dish sprayed with cooking spray; sprinkle with cheese. Bake at 325°F 30 minutes or until bubbly.

Makes 4 servings

Favorite recipe from **National Turkey Federation**

Turkey Florentine Spaghetti Pie

8 ounces spaghetti, uncooked
1 tablespoon low-fat margarine
½ cup *plus* 2 tablespoons grated
  Parmesan or Romano cheese, divided
1 egg, beaten slightly
  Nonstick cooking spray
1 pound ground turkey
1 tablespoon olive oil
½ cup chopped onion
1 clove garlic, chopped
1 (29-ounce) can tomatoes, undrained
  and coarsely chopped
1 (6-ounce) can tomato paste
1 tablespoon dried Italian seasoning
1 cup fat-free ricotta cheese
1½ teaspoons dried basil leaves *or*
  3 tablespoons finely chopped fresh
  basil
1 teaspoon dried parsley flakes *or*
  3 tablespoons chopped fresh parsley
  Dash of pepper
1 (10-ounce) package frozen chopped
  spinach, cooked and drained well
¾ cup (3 ounces) shredded low-fat
  mozzarella cheese
1 large *or* 2 medium fresh tomatoes

Break spaghetti in half; cook according to package directions. Drain well. Stir in margarine, ½ cup Parmesan cheese and egg. Cool about 5 minutes. Place spaghetti mixture in deep-dish 10-inch pie plate coated with cooking spray; press onto bottom and sides of pie plate to form crust. Set aside.

Brown turkey in olive oil in large skillet with onion and garlic, stirring to break meat into small pieces. Add canned tomatoes, tomato paste and Italian seasoning; bring to simmer and cook about 5 minutes, stirring frequently.

Mix ricotta cheese, basil, parsley flakes and pepper in small bowl; spoon into spaghetti crust. Cover with layers of spinach, turkey mixture and mozzarella cheese.

Slice fresh tomatoes into ½-inch-thick slices and arrange on top of mozzarella cheese. Sprinkle with remaining 2 tablespoons Parmesan cheese.

Bake uncovered 350°F 25 minutes or until heated through.   *Makes 6 servings*

Note: Baked pie can be frozen and reheated in microwave oven or refrigerated up to 3 days.

Favorite recipe from **North Dakota Wheat Commission**

Mexican Lasagna

½ pound lean ground turkey
½ cup chopped onion
½ cup chopped bell pepper
½ teaspoon black pepper
½ teaspoon dried basil leaves, crushed
1 can (8 ounces) low-sodium tomato
    sauce
1 cup GUILTLESS GOURMET® Salsa
    (mild, medium or hot), divided
1 cup low-fat cottage cheese
½ cup GUILTLESS GOURMET® Nacho
    Dip (mild or spicy)
   Nonstick cooking spray
1 bag (7 ounces) GUILTLESS
    GOURMET® Unsalted Baked Tortilla
    Chips, crushed

Preheat oven to 350°F. Cook turkey, onion, bell pepper, black pepper and basil in nonstick skillet over medium heat until turkey is no longer pink, breaking up meat and stirring occasionally. Stir in tomato sauce and ½ cup salsa; remove from heat. Combine cottage cheese and nacho dip in small bowl. Coat 11×7-inch baking dish with cooking spray. Set aside.

To assemble lasagna, place ⅓ of crushed chips in bottom of prepared dish, spreading to cover. Top with half the turkey mixture. Spread half the cheese mixture over turkey mixture. Repeat layers once. Top with remaining crushed chips; pour remaining salsa evenly over chips.

Bake 30 minutes or until heated through. Let stand 10 minutes before serving.   *Makes 4 servings*

Turkey Olé

½ cup minced onions
2 tablespoons butter or margarine
1 tablespoon all-purpose flour
1½ cups cubed cooked turkey
1½ cups prepared HIDDEN VALLEY
      RANCH® Original Ranch® Salad
      Dressing
3 ounces rotini, cooked according to
      package directions
½ (10-ounce) package frozen peas, thawed
⅓ cup canned diced green chiles, drained
1 teaspoon dried oregano, crushed
⅛ to ¼ teaspoon black pepper (optional)
3 tablespoons dry bread crumbs
1 tablespoon butter or margarine, melted
   Tomato wedges

Preheat oven to 350°F. In skillet, sauté onions in
2 tablespoons butter until tender. Stir in flour and
cook until smooth and bubbly; remove from heat. In
1½-quart casserole, combine turkey, salad dressing,
rotini, peas, chiles, oregano and pepper; stir in onion
mixture. In small bowl, combine bread crumbs with
melted butter; sprinkle over casserole. Bake until
heated through and bread crumbs are browned, 15 to
20 minutes. Garnish with tomato wedges.

Makes 6 servings

Turkey Tamale Pie with Cornbread

2 tablespoons vegetable oil
1 small onion, chopped
1 small green bell pepper, chopped
1¼ pounds turkey cutlets, diced
1 can (15¼ ounces) whole kernel corn, drained
1 can (15 ounces) kidney beans, drained
1 can (14½ ounces) stewed tomatoes
1 can (6 ounces) tomato paste
½ cup water
1 can (4 ounces) diced green chiles, drained
1 package (1 ounce) LAWRY'S® Taco Spices & Seasonings
1 package (16 ounces) cornbread mix

In large skillet, heat oil. Add onion and bell pepper; sauté 5 minutes. Add turkey; cook 7 to 10 minutes or until no longer pink in center, stirring occasionally. Reduce heat to low. Stir in corn, beans, stewed tomatoes, tomato paste, water, green chiles and Taco Spices & Seasonings. Simmer 10 minutes, stirring occasionally. Pour mixture into lightly greased 13×9-inch baking pan. In medium bowl, prepare cornbread batter according to package directions. Spoon dollops of batter over turkey mixture. Spoon remaining batter into lightly greased muffin tins. Bake in 375°F oven 25 minutes for casserole (15 to 20 minutes for muffins) or until toothpick inserted into cornbread comes out clean. *Makes 8 to 10 servings*

Mexican Turkey Rice

½ cup chopped onion
⅓ cup long-grain rice
1 clove garlic, minced
1 tablespoon olive oil
1 can (16 ounces) low-salt stewed
      tomatoes, coarsely chopped
½ cup reduced-sodium chicken broth
1 teaspoon chili powder
½ teaspoon dried oregano leaves
⅛ teaspoon crushed red pepper
⅓ cup chopped green bell pepper
1 pound fully-cooked oven-roasted turkey
      breast, cut into ¼-inch cubes

1. In large nonstick skillet over medium-high heat, cook and stir onion, rice and garlic in oil 3 to 4 minutes or until rice is lightly browned. Stir in tomatoes, broth, chili powder, oregano and crushed red pepper. Bring to a boil. Reduce heat to low; cover and simmer 15 minutes, stirring occasionally.

2. Stir in bell pepper and turkey. Cover; cook 3 to 4 minutes or until mixture is heated through.

Makes 6 servings

Favorite recipe from **National Turkey Federation**

Chicken and Zucchini Casserole

1¼ cups hot water
   3 tablespoons margarine or butter,
      divided
   3 cups STOVE TOP® Stuffing Mix for
      Chicken or Cornbread Stuffing Mix in
      the Canister
   ¾ pound boneless skinless chicken
      breasts, cubed
   2 medium zucchini, cut into ½-inch
      pieces
1½ cups (6 ounces) shredded Cheddar
      cheese
   1 can (8 ounces) water chestnuts,
      drained, halved (optional)
   ½ teaspoon dried basil leaves
   ¼ teaspoon pepper

MIX water and 2 tablespoons of the margarine in large bowl until margarine is melted. Stir in stuffing mix just to moisten.

PLACE chicken, zucchini and remaining 1 tablespoon margarine in 3-quart microwavable casserole. Cover loosely with waxed paper.

MICROWAVE on HIGH 4 minutes, stirring halfway through cooking time. Stir in prepared stuffing, cheese, water chestnuts, basil and pepper until well mixed. Cover.

MICROWAVE 10 minutes, stirring halfway through cooking time. Let stand 5 minutes.

Makes 6 servings

Marvelous

MEATS

Family Favorite Hamburger Casserole

- 1 tablespoon CRISCO® Vegetable Oil
- 1 cup chopped onion
- 1 pound ground beef round
- 1 package (9 ounces) frozen cut green beans
- 3 cups frozen southern-style hash brown potatoes
- 1 can (10¾ ounces) zesty tomato soup
- ½ cup water
- 1 teaspoon dried basil leaves
- ¾ teaspoon salt
- ¼ teaspoon pepper
- ¼ cup plain dry bread crumbs

1. Heat oven to 350°F. Oil 11¾×7½×2-inch baking dish lightly.

2. Heat 1 tablespoon Crisco® Oil in large skillet over medium-high heat. Add onion. Cook and stir until tender. Add meat. Cook until browned, stirring occasionally. Add beans. Cook and stir 5 minutes or until thawed. Add potatoes.

3. Combine tomato soup and water in small bowl. Stir until well blended. Stir into skillet. Stir in basil, salt and pepper. Spoon into baking dish. Sprinkle with bread crumbs.

4. Bake at 350°F for 30 minutes or until potatoes are tender. Let stand 5 minutes before serving.

Makes 4 servings

Oven-Easy Beef & Potato Dinner

4 cups frozen hash brown potatoes,
   thawed
3 tablespoons vegetable oil
⅛ teaspoon pepper
1 pound ground beef
1 cup water
1 package (about ¾ ounce) brown gravy
   mix
½ teaspoon garlic salt
1 package (10 ounces) frozen mixed
   vegetables, thawed and drained
1 cup (4 ounces) shredded Cheddar
   cheese
1⅓ cups (2.8 ounce can) FRENCH'S®
   French Fried Onions, divided

Preheat oven to 400°F. In 12×8-inch baking dish,
combine potatoes, oil and pepper. Firmly press potato
mixture evenly across bottom and up sides of dish to
form a shell. Bake, uncovered, at 400°F for 15 minutes.
Meanwhile, in large skillet, brown ground beef; drain.
Stir in water, gravy mix and garlic salt; bring to a boil.
Add mixed vegetables; reduce heat to medium and
cook, uncovered, 5 minutes. Remove from heat and stir
in ½ cup cheese and ⅔ cup French Fried Onions; spoon
into hot potato shell. Reduce oven temperature to
350°F. Bake, uncovered, at 350°F for 15 minutes or
until heated through. Top with remaining ½ cup cheese
and ⅔ cup onions; bake, uncovered, 5 minutes or until
onions are golden brown.   *Makes 4 to 6 servings*

Chop Suey Casserole

2 cups (12 ounces) cooked roast beef strips
1 can (10¾ ounces) condensed cream of mushroom soup
1 package (10 ounces) frozen French-style green beans, thawed and drained
1 can (8 ounces) sliced water chestnuts, drained
½ cup diagonally sliced celery
½ cup milk
2 tablespoons soy sauce
1⅓ cups (2.8 ounce can) FRENCH'S® French Fried Onions, divided
1 medium tomato, cut into wedges

Preheat oven to 350°F. In large bowl, combine beef, soup, beans, water chestnuts, celery, milk, soy sauce and ⅔ *cup* French Fried Onions. Spoon beef mixture into 1½-quart casserole. Bake, covered, at 350°F for 30 minutes or until heated through. Arrange tomato wedges around edge of casserole and top with remaining ⅔ *cup* onions. Bake, uncovered, 5 minutes or until onions are golden brown.   *Makes 4 servings*

Microwave Directions: Prepare beef mixture as directed; spoon into 1½-quart microwave-safe casserole. Cook, covered, on HIGH 10 to 12 minutes or until heated through, stirring beef mixture halfway through cooking time. Top with tomato wedges and remaining onions as directed; cook, uncovered, 1 minute. Let stand 5 minutes.

Countdown Casserole

1 jar (8 ounces) pasteurized process
   cheese spread
¾ cup milk
1 bag (16 ounces) frozen vegetable
   combination (broccoli, corn, red
   pepper), thawed and drained
4 cups frozen hash brown potatoes,
   thawed
2 cups (12 ounces) cubed cooked roast
   beef
1⅓ cups (2.8 ounce can) FRENCH'S®
   French Fried Onions, divided
½ teaspoon seasoned salt
¼ teaspoon freshly ground black pepper
½ cup (2 ounces) shredded Cheddar
   cheese

Preheat oven to 375°F. Spoon cheese spread into
12×8-inch baking dish; place in oven just until cheese
melts, about 5 minutes. Using fork, stir milk into
melted cheese until well blended. Stir in vegetables,
potatoes, beef, ⅔ *cup* French Fried Onions and
seasonings. Bake, covered, at 375°F 30 minutes or
until heated through. Top with Cheddar cheese;
sprinkle remaining ⅔ *cup* onions down center. Bake,
uncovered, 3 minutes or until onions are golden
brown.   *Makes 4 to 6 servings*

Microwave Directions: In 12×8-inch microwave-safe dish, combine cheese spread and milk. Cook, covered, on HIGH 3 minutes; stir. Add ingredients as directed. Cook, covered, 14 minutes or until heated through, stirring beef mixture halfway through cooking time. Top with Cheddar cheese and remaining onions as directed. Cook, uncovered, 1 minute or until cheese melts. Let stand 5 minutes.

French Veal Casserole

1 **pound veal steaks**
2 **tablespoons salad oil**
1 **cup rice**
1 **tablespoon chopped onion**
2¼ **cups water**
2 **teaspoons salt**
2 **tablespoons chopped pimiento**
½ **cup BLUE DIAMOND® Slivered Almonds, toasted**

Cut meat into ½-inch cubes. Brown lightly in oil in large skillet. Remove meat from skillet. Combine rice and onion in same pan; cook, stirring, until rice is golden brown. Add water and salt; bring to boil. Stir in veal. Spoon into casserole dish; cover. Bake at 300°F 50 to 60 minutes or until rice and veal are tender. Just before serving, add pimiento and almonds; fluff with fork. *Makes 6 servings*

Speedy Stuffed Peppers

4   red, green or yellow bell peppers
¾   pound lean ground beef (80% lean)
⅓   cup chopped onion
1   clove garlic, minced
1   package (6.8 ounces) RICE-A-RONI®
      Beef Flavor
¼   cup tomato paste
¼   cup water
1   tablespoon brown sugar
3   tablespoons grated Parmesan cheese
      (optional)

1. Cut peppers in half lengthwise; remove seeds and membranes. Cook in boiling water 5 minutes; drain well. (Or, microwave in 13×9-inch glass baking dish, covered with plastic wrap, 5 minutes on HIGH.)

2. In large skillet, brown ground beef, onion and garlic; drain. Remove from skillet; set aside.

3. In same skillet, prepare Rice-A-Roni® mix as package directs.

4. Heat oven to 375°F. Place cooked peppers cut-side up in 13×9-inch glass baking dish. Combine rice and meat mixture; spoon into pepper halves. Combine tomato paste, water and brown sugar; spoon over rice mixture.

5. Tent peppers with foil; bake 25 to 30 minutes or until heated through. Sprinkle with cheese, if desired.

Makes 4 servings

Chunky Chili Casserole

2 cups STOVE TOP® Stuffing Mix for
Chicken or Cornbread Stuffing Mix in
the Canister
½ cup hot water
½ pound ground beef
1 small onion, chopped
1 can (15 ounces) chili with beans
1½ cups (6 ounces) shredded Cheddar
cheese, divided
½ cup frozen sweet corn, thawed
¼ cup sliced pitted ripe olives

MIX stuffing mix and hot water in 2-quart microwavable casserole. Spread evenly in casserole.

MIX meat and onion in large microwavable bowl. Cover loosely with waxed paper.

MICROWAVE on HIGH 4 minutes or until meat is no longer pink. Drain. Stir in chili, 1 cup cheese, corn and olives. Spoon over stuffing. Cover loosely with wax paper.

MICROWAVE 10 minutes, rotating casserole halfway through cooking time. Let stand 5 minutes. Sprinkle with remaining ½ cup cheese. Serve with BREAKSTONE'S® or KNUDSEN® Sour Cream.

Makes 4 servings

Note: Recipe can also be prepared in 4 individual 1½-cup microwavable dishes. Microwave each dish on HIGH 3 minutes or until heated through.

Texas-Style Deep-Dish Chili Pie

- 1 **pound beef stew meat, cut into ½-inch cubes**
- 1 **tablespoon vegetable oil**
- 2 **cans (14½ ounces each) Mexican-style stewed tomatoes, undrained**
- 1 **medium green bell pepper, diced**
- 1 **package (1 ounce) LAWRY'S® Taco Spices & Seasonings**
- 1 **tablespoon yellow cornmeal**
- 1 **can (15¼ ounces) kidney beans, drained**
- 1 **package (15 ounces) refrigerated flat pie crusts**
- ½ **cup (2 ounces) shredded Cheddar cheese, divided**

In Dutch oven, brown beef in oil; drain fat. Add stewed tomatoes, bell pepper, Taco Spices & Seasonings and cornmeal. Bring to a boil; reduce heat and simmer, uncovered, 20 minutes. Add kidney beans.

In 10-inch pie plate, unfold 1 crust and fill with chili mixture and ¼ cup cheese. Top with remaining crust, fluting edges. Bake, uncovered, in 350°F oven 30 minutes. Sprinkle remaining cheese over crust; return to oven and bake 10 minutes longer.

Makes 6 servings

Old-Fashioned Beef Pot Pie

1   pound ground beef
1   can (11 ounces) condensed beef with
     vegetables and barley soup
½   cup water
1   package (10 ounces) frozen peas and
     carrots, thawed and drained
½   teaspoon seasoned salt
⅛   teaspoon garlic powder
⅛   teaspoon ground black pepper
1   cup (4 ounces) shredded Cheddar
     cheese
1⅓ cups (2.8 ounce can) FRENCH'S®
     French Fried Onions, divided
1   package (7.5 ounces) refrigerated
     biscuits

Preheat oven to 350°F. In large skillet, brown ground beef in large chunks; drain. Stir in soup, water, vegetables and seasonings; bring to a boil. Reduce heat and simmer, uncovered, 5 minutes. Remove from heat; stir in ½ *cup* cheese and ⅔ *cup* French Fried Onions.

Pour mixture into 12×8-inch baking dish. Cut each biscuit in half; place, cut side down, around edge of casserole. Bake, uncovered, 15 to 20 minutes or until biscuits are done. Top with remaining ½ *cup* cheese and ⅔ *cup* onions; bake, uncovered, 5 minutes or until onions are golden brown.   *Makes 4 to 6 servings*

Taco Bake

TACO MEAT FILLING
- 1 pound ground beef
- ½ cup chopped onion
- 1 package (about 1⅛ ounces) taco
  seasoning mix

TACO CRUST
- 1¾ to 2 cups all-purpose flour, divided
- 1 package RED STAR® Active Dry Yeast
  or QUICK-RISE™ Yeast
- 1 tablespoon sugar
- 2 teaspoons finely chopped onion
- ¾ teaspoon salt
- ⅔ cup warm water
- 2 tablespoons oil
- ½ cup crushed corn chips

TOPPINGS
- 1 cup shredded Cheddar cheese
- 1 cup shredded lettuce
- 1½ cups chopped tomatoes

Brown ground beef with ½ cup onion; drain. Add taco
seasoning. Prepare taco filling according to seasoning
packet directions.

Preheat oven to 375°F. In medium mixing bowl,
combine 1 cup flour, yeast, sugar, 2 teaspoons onion
and salt; mix well. Add warm water (120° to 130°F) and
oil to flour mixture. Mix by hand until almost smooth.
Stir in corn chips and enough remaining flour to make
a stiff batter. Spread into well-greased 10-inch pie pan,
forming a rim around edge. Cover; let rise in warm

place about 20 minutes (10 minutes for QUICK-RISE™ Yeast). Spread meat filling over dough. Bake at 375°F 30 to 35 minutes or until edge is crisp and light golden brown. Sprinkle with cheese, lettuce and tomatoes. Serve immediately.   *Makes 4 to 6 servings*

Steak Pot Pie

- 1 **cup chopped onion**
- 2 **tablespoons margarine**
- 3 **tablespoons all-purpose flour**
- 1½ **cups COLLEGE INN® Beef Broth**
- ½ **cup A.1. ORIGINAL® or A.1. BOLD® Steak Sauce**
- 3 **cups cubed cooked steak (about 1½ pounds)**
- 1 **(16-ounce) package frozen broccoli, cauliflower & carrot mixture**
  Prepared pastry for 1-crust pie
- 1 **egg, beaten**

In 2-quart saucepan, over medium-high heat, cook onion in margarine until tender. Blend in flour; cook 1 minute more. Add broth and steak sauce; cook and stir until mixture thickens and begins to boil. Stir in steak and vegetables. Spoon mixture into 8-inch square glass baking dish. Roll out and cut pastry crust to fit over dish. Seal crust to edge of dish; brush with egg. Slit top of crust to vent. Bake at 400°F 25 minutes or until crust is golden brown. Serve immediately.

Makes 4 servings

Heartland Shepherd's Pie

¾ pound ground beef
1 medium onion, chopped
1 can (14½ ounces) DEL MONTE®
   FreshCut™ Diced Tomatoes with
   Green Pepper & Onion Original
   Recipe Stewed Tomatoes
1 can (8 ounces) DEL MONTE® Tomato
   Sauce
1 can (14½ ounces) DEL MONTE® Mixed
   Vegetables, drained
   Instant mashed potato flakes plus
   ingredients to prepare (enough for
   6 servings)
3 cloves garlic, minced

1. Preheat oven to 375°F. In large skillet, brown meat and onion over medium-high heat; drain.

2. Add tomatoes and tomato sauce; cook over high heat until thickened, stirring frequently. Stir in mixed vegetables. Season with salt and pepper, if desired. Spoon into 2-quart baking dish; set aside.

3. Prepare 6 servings mashed potatoes according to package directions, first cooking garlic in specified amount of butter.

4. Top meat mixture with potatoes. Bake 20 minutes or until heated through.   *Makes 4 to 6 servings*

Twisty Beef Bake

1 **pound ground beef**
2 **cups rotini or elbow macaroni, cooked in unsalted water and drained**
1⅓ **cups (2.8 ounce can) FRENCH'S® French Fried Onions, divided**
1 **cup (4 ounces) shredded Cheddar cheese, divided**
1 **can (14½ ounces) whole tomatoes, undrained and chopped**
1 **can (10¾ ounces) condensed cream of mushroom soup, undiluted**
¼ **cup chopped green bell pepper**
¼ **teaspoon seasoned salt**

Preheat oven to 375°F. In large skillet, brown ground beef; drain. Stir in hot macaroni, ⅔ *cup* French Fried Onions, ½ *cup* cheese, tomatoes, soup, bell pepper and seasoned salt. Mix well. Pour into 2-quart casserole. Bake, covered, for 30 minutes or until heated through. Top with remaining ½ *cup* cheese and ⅔ *cup* onions; bake, uncovered, 3 minutes or until onions are golden brown. *Makes 4 to 6 servings*

Microwave Directions: Crumble ground beef into 2-quart microwave-safe casserole. Cook, covered, on HIGH 4 to 6 minutes or until beef is cooked. Stir beef halfway through cooking time. Drain well. Add remaining ingredients as above. Cook, covered, 10 to 14 minutes or until heated through. Stir beef mixture halfway through cooking time. Top with remaining cheese and onions; cook, uncovered, 1 minute or until cheese melts. Let stand 5 minutes.

Johnnie Marzetti

1 tablespoon CRISCO® Vegetable Oil
1 cup chopped celery
1 cup chopped onion
1 medium green bell pepper, chopped
1 pound ground beef round
1 can (14½ ounces) Italian-style stewed tomatoes
1 can (8 ounces) tomato sauce
1 can (6 ounces) tomato paste
1 cup water
1 bay leaf
1½ teaspoons dried basil leaves
1¼ teaspoons salt
¼ teaspoon black pepper
1 package (12 ounces) egg noodles, cooked and well drained
1 cup (4 ounces) shredded sharp Cheddar cheese
½ cup plain dry bread crumbs

1. Heat oven to 375°F. Lightly oil 12½×8½×2-inch baking dish.

2. Heat 1 tablespoon Crisco® Oil in large skillet on medium heat. Add celery, onion and green pepper. Cook and stir until tender. Remove vegetables from skillet. Set aside. Add meat to skillet. Cook until browned, stirring occasionally. Return vegetables to skillet. Add tomatoes, tomato sauce, tomato paste, water, bay leaf, basil, salt and black pepper. Reduce heat to low. Simmer 5 minutes, stirring occasionally. Remove bay leaf; discard.

3. Place noodles in baking dish. Spoon meat mixture over noodles. Sprinkle with cheese and bread crumbs.

4. Bake at 375°F for 15 to 20 minutes or until cheese melts. Garnish, if desired. *Makes 8 servings*

Crazy Lasagna Casserole

1½ pounds ground beef
1 can (8 ounces) tomato sauce
1 can (6 ounces) tomato paste
1½ cups water
1 package (1½ ounces) LAWRY'S®
      Original-Style Spaghetti Sauce
      Spices & Seasonings
1 teaspoon LAWRY'S® Seasoned Salt
1 package (10 ounces) medium-size shell
      macaroni, cooked and drained
1 carton (16 ounces) small curd cottage
      cheese
1½ cups (6 ounces) shredded Cheddar cheese

In large skillet, brown beef until crumbly; drain fat. Add tomato sauce, tomato paste, water, Original-Style Spaghetti Sauce Spices & Seasonings and Seasoned Salt. Blend well. Bring to a boil; reduce heat and simmer, uncovered, 10 minutes, stirring occasionally. In shallow 2-quart casserole, layer half of macaroni, cottage cheese and sauce. Sprinkle ½ cup Cheddar cheese over sauce. Repeat layers, ending with meat sauce. Top with remaining 1 cup Cheddar cheese. Bake, uncovered, in 350°F oven 30 to 40 minutes or until bubbly and cheese is melted. *Makes 8 servings*

Bistro Burgundy Stew

1 pound boneless beef sirloin, cut into
  1½-inch pieces
3 tablespoons all-purpose flour
6 slices bacon, cut into 1-inch pieces
  (about ¼ pound)
2 cloves garlic, crushed
3 carrots, peeled and cut into 1-inch
  pieces (about 1½ cups)
¾ cup Burgundy or other dry red wine
½ cup GREY POUPON® Dijon Mustard
½ cup COLLEGE INN® Beef Broth or
  Lower Sodium Beef Broth
12 small mushrooms
1½ cups green onions, cut into 1½-inch
  pieces

Coat beef with flour, shaking off excess; set aside.

In large skillet, over medium heat, cook bacon just
until done; pour off excess fat. Add beef and garlic;
cook until browned. Add carrots, wine, mustard and
beef broth. Heat to a boil; reduce heat. Cover; simmer
for 30 minutes or until carrots are tender, stirring
occasionally. Stir in mushrooms and green onions;
cook 10 minutes more, stirring occasionally.

Makes 4 servings

Beef Burgundy Stew

1 (1-pound) boneless beef sirloin steak,
  cut into 1½-inch cubes
3 tablespoons all-purpose flour
6 slices bacon, cut into 1-inch pieces
  (about ¼ pound)
1 large onion, cut into wedges (about
  1½ cups)
3 carrots, peeled, cut into ½-inch pieces
  (about 1½ cups)
12 small fresh mushrooms
1 cup Burgundy or other dry red wine
½ cup A.1. ORIGINAL® or A.1. BOLD®
  Steak Sauce
2 cloves garlic, minced

Coat beef with flour, shaking off excess; set aside.

In 6-quart pot, over medium heat, cook bacon until
crisp; remove with slotted spoon. Set aside.

In same pot, brown beef, a few pieces at a time, in
drippings. Return bacon to pot; stir in onion, carrots,
mushrooms, wine, steak sauce and garlic. Cover;
simmer 40 minutes or until carrots are tender, stirring
occasionally. Serve immediately.

Makes 6 servings

French Beef Stew

1½ pounds stew beef, cut into 1-inch cubes
¼ cup all-purpose flour
2 tablespoons vegetable oil
2 cans (14½ ounces each) DEL MONTE®
     FreshCut™ Diced Tomatoes with
     Garlic & Onion Original Recipe
     Stewed Tomatoes
1 can (14 ounces) beef broth
4 medium carrots, peeled and cut into
     1-inch chunks
2 medium potatoes, peeled and cut into
     1-inch chunks
¾ teaspoon dried thyme, crushed
2 tablespoons Dijon mustard (optional)

1. Combine meat and flour in large plastic food storage bag; toss to coat evenly.

2. Brown meat in hot oil in 6-quart saucepan. Season with salt and pepper, if desired.

3. Add all remaining ingredients except mustard. Bring to boil; reduce heat to medium-low. Cover; simmer 1 hour or until beef is tender.

4. Blend in mustard. Garnish and serve with warm crusty French bread, if desired.

Makes 6 to 8 servings

Hungarian Goulash Stew

¾ pound lean ground beef (80% lean)
½ cup chopped onion
1 clove garlic, minced
1 package (4.8 ounces) PASTA RONI®
   Angel Hair Pasta with Herbs
1 can (14½ ounces) diced tomatoes,
   undrained
1 cup frozen corn *or* 1 can (8 ounces)
   whole kernel corn, drained
1½ teaspoons paprika
⅛ teaspoon black pepper
   Sour cream (optional)

1. In 3-quart saucepan, brown ground beef, onion and garlic; drain.

2. Add 1⅓ cups water, pasta, contents of seasoning packet, tomatoes and juices, frozen corn and seasonings. Bring just to a boil.

3. Reduce heat to medium.

4. Boil, uncovered, stirring frequently, 5 to 6 minutes or until pasta is tender.

5. Let stand 3 minutes or until desired consistency. Stir before serving. Serve with sour cream, if desired.

Makes 4 servings

Jalapeño Two-Bean Chili

1 tablespoon vegetable oil
1 medium onion, chopped
1 green bell pepper, seeded and chopped
2 cloves garlic, minced
1 can (16 ounces) pinto beans, rinsed
  and drained
1 can (16 ounces) black beans, rinsed
  and drained
1 can (14½ ounces) stewed tomatoes or
  Mexican-style stewed tomatoes,
  undrained
1 can (10½ ounces) kosher condensed
  beef or chicken broth
½ cup water
2 teaspoons chili powder
2 teaspoons ground cumin
1 to 2 teaspoons chopped bottled or fresh
  jalapeño peppers
1 package (12 ounces) HEBREW
  NATIONAL® Beef Hot Sausage or
  Lean Smoked Turkey Sausage
  Chopped cilantro (optional)
  Diced avocado (optional)

Heat oil in large saucepan over medium heat. Add
onion, bell pepper and garlic; cook 8 minutes, stirring
occasionally. Add pinto and black beans, tomatoes with
liquid, broth, water, chili powder, cumin and jalapeño
peppers; bring to a boil. Cut sausage into ½-inch slices.

Cut slices into quarters. Stir in sausage; reduce heat to medium-low. Simmer, uncovered, 15 minutes, stirring occasionally. Ladle into shallow bowls; top with cilantro and avocado, if desired.

Makes 6 servings

Vegetable-Beef Chili

1   (1-pound) beef top round or chuck
      steak, cut into ¼-inch cubes
1   tablespoon vegetable oil
1   cup coarsely chopped green bell pepper
½   cup coarsely chopped onion
1   clove garlic, minced
3   to 4 tablespoons chili powder
2   (16-ounce) cans tomatoes, undrained,
      coarsely chopped
¾   cup A.1. ORIGINAL® or A.1. BOLD®
      Steak Sauce
1   (17-ounce) can corn, drained
1   (15-ounce) can kidney beans, drained

In 6-quart pot, over medium-high heat, brown steak in oil; drain, if necessary. Reduce heat to medium; add pepper, onion and garlic. Cook and stir until vegetables are tender, about 3 minutes. Mix in chili powder; cook and stir 1 minute. Add tomatoes with liquid and steak sauce; heat to a boil. Reduce heat. Cover; simmer 45 minutes, stirring occasionally. Add corn and beans; simmer 15 minutes more or until steak is tender. Serve immediately.   *Makes 6 servings*

Meatball Stroganoff with Rice

MEATBALLS

1½   pounds ground beef round
⅓   cup plain dry bread crumbs
1   egg, lightly beaten
1   tablespoon Worcestershire sauce
1   teaspoon salt
¼   teaspoon pepper
2   tablespoons CRISCO® Vegetable Oil

SAUCE

1   tablespoon CRISCO® Vegetable Oil
½   pound mushrooms, sliced
2   tablespoons all-purpose flour
1   teaspoon ketchup
1   can (10½ ounces) condensed, double
     strength beef broth (bouillon),
     undiluted*
½   (1-ounce) envelope dry onion soup mix
     (about 2 tablespoons)
1   cup sour cream
4   cups hot cooked rice

1. *For meatballs,* combine meat, bread crumbs, egg, Worcestershire sauce, salt and pepper in large bowl. Mix until well blended. Shape into eighteen 2-inch meatballs.

2. Heat 2 tablespoons Crisco® Oil in large skillet over medium heat. Add meatballs. Brown on all sides. Reduce heat to low. Cook 10 minutes. Remove meatballs from skillet.

3. *For sauce,* add 1 tablespoon Crisco® Oil to skillet. Add mushrooms. Cook and stir 4 minutes. Remove skillet from heat.

4. Stir in flour and ketchup until blended. Stir in broth gradually. Add soup mix. Return to heat. Bring to a boil over medium heat. Reduce heat to low. Simmer 2 minutes. Return meatballs to skillet. Heat thoroughly, stirring occasionally.

5. Stir in sour cream. Heat but do not bring to a boil. Serve over hot rice.   *Makes 6 servings*

*1¼ cups reconstituted beef broth made with double amount of very low sodium beef broth granules may be substituted for beef broth (bouillon).

Thai Beef and Noodle Toss

1   pound beef round tip steaks, cut ⅛ to
    ¼ inch thick
1   to 2 jalapeño peppers,* minced
2   cloves garlic, minced
2   tablespoons Oriental sesame oil, divided
1   (3-ounce) package beef-flavored instant
    ramen noodles
1   cup diagonally sliced carrots
½   cup chopped green onions
½   cup A.1. THICK & HEARTY® Steak
    Sauce
¼   cup water
¼   cup PLANTERS® Unsalted Peanuts,
    chopped
2   tablespoons chopped fresh cilantro or
    parsley

Cut steaks crosswise into 1-inch-wide strips; cut each strip in half. In large bowl, toss steaks, jalapeños and garlic with 1 tablespoon oil; set aside.

Break noodles into 3 or 4 pieces; set aside seasoning packet. Cook noodles according to package directions; drain and rinse. Meanwhile, heat large skillet or wok over medium-high heat; stir-fry reserved steak mixture in batches 30 to 60 seconds or until steak is desired doneness. Remove steak mixture from skillet; keep warm.

In same skillet, in remaining 1 tablespoon oil, stir-fry carrots and green onions until tender. Add cooked noodles, steak sauce, water, peanuts and cilantro;

sprinkle with reserved seasoning packet. Heat mixture until hot, stirring occasionally. Return warm steak mixture to skillet; mix lightly. Serve immediately.

Makes 4 servings

*Remove interior ribs and seeds if a milder flavor is desired.

Quick Skillet Supper

½ pound beef sirloin steak
1 tablespoon vegetable oil
1 can (17 ounces) whole kernel corn, drained
1 can (14½ ounces) stewed tomatoes, undrained
2 cups (about 8 ounces) sliced fresh mushrooms
1 clove garlic, minced
1 teaspoon dried oregano leaves
⅛ teaspoon ground black pepper
3 cups hot cooked rice

Partially freeze steak; slice across the grain into ⅛-inch strips. Heat oil in large skillet over medium-high heat until hot. Brown meat quickly in oil, about 2 minutes; remove. Add vegetables, garlic, oregano and pepper; stir. Reduce heat to medium; cover and cook 5 minutes. Add meat and cook until heated. Serve over rice.

Makes 6 servings

Favorite recipe from **USA Rice Council**

Corned Beef Hash

6   to 7 medium red boiling potatoes, peeled
1   teaspoon salt, divided
3   tablespoons parve margarine
1   cup chopped onion
⅓   cup chopped red bell pepper
¼   teaspoon freshly ground black pepper
2   cups chopped cooked **HEBREW NATIONAL®** Corned Beef

Place potatoes in medium saucepan; cover with water. Cover; bring to a boil over high heat. Add ¼ teaspoon salt. Boil 12 to 15 minutes or until fork-tender. Drain; rinse with cold water. Cut potatoes into ½-inch pieces.

Melt margarine in large nonstick skillet over medium heat. Add onion and bell pepper; cook and stir 5 minutes. Add potatoes, remaining ¾ teaspoon salt and black pepper; cook, stirring occasionally, 15 minutes or until browned. Stir corned beef into potato mixture. Cook 3 minutes or until heated through.

Makes 4 servings

Shepherd's Pie

2 **cups diced cooked leg of American lamb**
2 **cups prepared brown gravy**
2 **large potatoes, cubed and cooked**
1 **cup cooked peas**
1 **cup cooked carrot slices**
3 **green onions, sliced**
1 **clove garlic, minced**
1 **teaspoon black pepper**
2 **sheets prepared pie dough***

In large bowl, combine lamb, brown gravy, potatoes, peas, carrots, green onions, garlic and pepper.

Press 1 sheet pie dough into 9-inch pie plate; fill with lamb mixture. Cover with second sheet of pie dough. Crimp edges; cut slits in top to allow steam to escape.

Bake 30 minutes at 350°F or until pie crust is golden brown. *Makes 4 to 6 servings*

*Or, use mashed potatoes on top in place of second crust.

Favorite recipe from **American Lamb Council**

Lamb & Pork Cassoulet

 1 **package (1 pound) dried white navy
      beans, rinsed**
 ½ **pound salt pork, sliced**
1½ **pounds boneless lamb shoulder or leg,
      cut into 1-inch cubes**
 4 **large pork chops**
 ½ **pound pork sausage links**
    Salt
    Pepper
 2 **large onions, chopped**
 1 **can (28 ounces) tomatoes, drained**
 ½ **cup dry red wine**
 ¼ **cup chopped fresh parsley**
 3 **cloves garlic, finely chopped**
 1 **teaspoon dried thyme, crushed**
 1 **bay leaf**

Place beans in large bowl. Cover with cold water; soak
overnight. Drain and rinse beans. Place beans in Dutch
oven; cover with cold water. Bring to a boil over high heat,
skimming foam as necessary. Reduce heat to low. Cover;
simmer about 1 hour. Drain beans; reserve liquid.

Cook salt pork in large skillet over medium-high heat
until some of fat is rendered. Remove salt pork. In
batches, brown lamb, pork chops and sausage in fat.
Remove meats from skillet; drain on paper towels. Cut
chops and sausage into 1-inch pieces. Sprinkle meat
with salt and pepper. Remove all but 2 tablespoons of
fat from skillet. Add onions. Cook and stir over
medium-high heat until onions are tender. Add
tomatoes, wine, parsley, garlic, thyme and bay leaf.

Combine tomato mixture, drained beans and meats in large bowl. Spoon into large casserole. Pour reserved bean liquid over mixture just to cover. Bake at 350°F about 1½ hours or until meat is fork-tender. Remove and discard bay leaf before serving.

Makes 6 to 8 servings

Favorite recipe from **American Lamb Council**

Dijon Lamb Stew

- ½ **pound boneless lamb, cut into small pieces***
- ½ **medium onion, chopped**
- ½ **teaspoon dried rosemary**
- 1 **tablespoon olive oil**
- 1 **can (14½ ounces) DEL MONTE® *FreshCut™* Diced Tomatoes with Basil, Garlic & Oregano**
- 1 **carrot, julienne cut**
- 1 **tablespoon Dijon mustard**
- 1 **can (15 ounces) white beans or pinto beans, drained**

1. Brown meat with onion and rosemary in oil in large skillet over medium-high heat, stirring occasionally. Season with salt and pepper, if desired.

2. Add tomatoes, carrot and mustard. Cover and cook over medium heat, 10 minutes; add beans.

3. Cook, uncovered, over medium heat 5 minutes, stirring occasionally. *Makes 4 servings*

*Top sirloin steak may be substituted for lamb.

Lamb & Green Chilie Stew

1 **pound boneless lean lamb, cubed**
1 **large onion, halved and sliced**
6 **cloves garlic, chopped or sliced**
2 **cans (15 ounces each) no-salt-added whole tomatoes, undrained**
1 **pound potatoes**
3 **cans (4 ounces each) diced mild green chilies**
2 **teaspoons dried rosemary**
1 **teaspoon dried oregano leaves**
1 **pound zucchini**
1 **cup frozen corn, thawed and drained Pickled jalapeño peppers (optional)**

1. Combine ½ cup water, lamb, onion and garlic in large saucepan. Bring to a simmer over medium-high heat. Cover; simmer 30 minutes or until onion is tender. Increase heat to high; uncover. Boil, stirring occasionally, until liquid evaporates and meat browns. Add tomatoes with liquid; stir. Reduce heat to medium-low. Cover; simmer 30 minutes.

2. Meanwhile, cut potatoes into 1½-inch pieces. Add potatoes, chilies, rosemary and oregano. Cover; simmer 20 to 30 minutes or until potatoes and lamb are tender.

3. Halve zucchini lengthwise and cut crosswise into ½- to ¾-inch pieces. Add zucchini and corn to stew. Cover; simmer 10 minutes or until zucchini is crisp-tender. Season with pepper. Garnish with jalapeños, if desired. *Makes 6 servings*

Spring Lamb Skillet

2　teaspoons olive oil
1　pound boneless lamb, cut into 1-inch
　　cubes
2　cups thinly sliced yellow squash
2　cups (about 8 ounces) sliced fresh
　　mushrooms
2　medium tomatoes, seeded and chopped
½　cup sliced green onions
3　cups cooked brown rice
½　teaspoon dried rosemary leaves
½　teaspoon salt
½　teaspoon ground black pepper

Heat oil in large skillet over medium heat until hot.
Add lamb and cook 3 to 5 minutes or until lamb is
browned. Remove from skillet; reserve. Add squash,
mushrooms, tomatoes and onions; cook 2 to
3 minutes or until vegetables are tender. Stir in rice,
rosemary, salt, pepper and reserved lamb. Cook until
thoroughly heated. *Makes 6 servings*

Ham Starburst Casserole

1   can (16 ounces) sliced potatoes,
     drained
1   can (10¾ ounces) condensed cream of
     potato soup
1   package (10 ounces) frozen peas,
     thawed and drained
¾   cup sour cream
1⅓ cup (2.8 ounce can) FRENCH'S®
     French Fried Onions, divided
2   tablespoons diced pimiento (optional)
8   to 12 ounces cooked ham or turkey
     ham, unsliced

Preheat oven to 350°F. In medium bowl, combine
potatoes, soup, peas, sour cream, ⅔ *cup* French Fried
Onions and pimiento; stir well. Spoon into 10-inch
round baking dish. Cut ham into 3 thick slices; cut
each slice crosswise into halves. Press ham slices into
potato mixture, rounded-side up in spoke-fashion, to
form a starburst. Bake, covered, at 350°F for 30
minutes or until heated through. Top with remaining
⅔ *cup* onions; bake, uncovered, 5 minutes or until
onions are golden brown.   *Makes 4 servings*

Tomato, Bacon and Cheese Supper

        1   medium onion, chopped
        2   tablespoons margarine or butter
        1   cup ricotta cheese
        1   cup milk
        3   eggs, well beaten
        3   cups STOVE TOP® Stuffing Mix for
              Chicken or Cornbread Stuffing Mix in
              the Canister
        1   cup (4 ounces) KRAFT® Natural
              Shredded Swiss Cheese, divided
        2   large tomatoes, chopped
        8   slices OSCAR MAYER® Bacon, crisply
              cooked and crumbled
       ¼   teaspoon pepper

PLACE onion and margarine in 3-quart microwavable
casserole. Cover loosely with waxed paper.

MICROWAVE on HIGH 3 minutes. Stir in ricotta
cheese, milk and eggs. Stir in stuffing mix, ¾ cup Swiss
cheese, tomatoes, bacon and pepper until well mixed.
Cover loosely with waxed paper.

MICROWAVE 10 minutes, stirring halfway through
cooking time. Sprinkle with remaining ¼ cup Swiss
cheese. Let stand 5 minutes.   *Makes 6 servings*

Stuffed Franks 'n Taters

- 4 cups frozen hash brown potatoes, thawed
- 1 can (10¾ ounces) condensed cream of celery soup
- 1 cup (4 ounces) shredded Cheddar cheese, divided
- 1 cup sour cream
- 1⅓ cups (2.8 ounce can) FRENCH'S® French Fried Onions, divided
- ½ teaspoon salt
- ¼ teaspoon pepper
- 6 frankfurters

Preheat oven to 400°F. In large bowl, combine potatoes, soup, *½ cup* cheese, sour cream, *⅔ cup* French Fried Onions and seasonings. Spread potato mixture in 12×8-inch baking dish. Split frankfurters lengthwise almost into halves. Arrange frankfurters, split-side up, along center of casserole. Bake, covered, at 400°F for 30 minutes or until heated through. Fill frankfurters with remaining *½ cup* cheese and *⅔ cup* onions; bake, uncovered, 1 to 3 minutes or until onions are golden brown.   *Makes 6 servings*

Microwave Directions: Prepare potato mixture as above; spread in 12×8-inch microwave-safe dish. Cook, covered, on HIGH 8 minutes, stirring halfway through cooking time. Split frankfurters and arrange on potatoes as directed. Cook, covered, 4 to 6 minutes or until frankfurters are heated through, rotating dish halfway through cooking time. Fill frankfurters with remaining cheese and onions; cook, uncovered, 1 minute or until cheese melts. Let stand 5 minutes.

Prize Potluck Casserole

1 cup lentils, rinsed and drained
2 cups water
1 can (16 ounces) tomatoes
¼ cup minced onion
¼ cup chopped green bell pepper
1 teaspoon salt
½ teaspoon dry mustard
¼ teaspoon Worcestershire sauce
¼ teaspoon ground black pepper
⅛ teaspoon dried thyme leaves
1 pound Polish sausage, cut into
    1½-inch-thick slices

Cook lentils in water in medium saucepan until tender, about 30 minutes; drain if necessary. Combine lentils with tomatoes, onion, green pepper and seasonings; spoon into 13×9-inch casserole. Top with sausage; cover. Bake at 350°F for 45 minutes. Remove cover; continue baking 15 minutes longer.

Makes 6 servings

Favorite recipe from **USA Dry Pea & Lentil Council**

Pork Chops O'Brien

- 1 tablespoon vegetable oil
- 6 pork chops, ½ to ¾ inch thick
   Seasoned salt
- 1 can (10¾ ounces) condensed cream of
   celery soup
- ½ cup milk
- ½ cup sour cream
- ½ teaspoon seasoned salt
- ¼ teaspoon pepper
- 1 bag (24 ounces) frozen O'Brien or hash
   brown potatoes, thawed
- 1 cup (4 ounces) shredded Cheddar
   cheese, divided
- 1⅓ cups (2.8 ounce can) FRENCH'S®
   French Fried Onions, divided

Preheat oven to 350°F. In large skillet, heat oil. Brown
pork chops on both sides; drain. Sprinkle chops with
seasoned salt; set aside. In large bowl, combine soup,
milk, sour cream, salt and pepper. Stir in potatoes,
½ cup cheese and *⅔ cup* French Fried Onions. Spoon
mixture into 13×9-inch baking dish; arrange pork
chops on top. Bake, covered, at 350°F for 35 to 40
minutes or until pork chops are done. Top chops with
remaining *½ cup* cheese and *⅔ cup* onions; bake,
uncovered, 5 minutes or until onions are golden
brown.   *Makes 6 servings*

Savory Pork Chop Supper

6 **medium potatoes, thinly sliced (about 5 cups)**

1⅓ **cups (2.8 ounce can) FRENCH'S® French Fried Onions, divided**

1 **jar (2 ounces) sliced mushrooms, drained**

2 **tablespoons butter or margarine**

¼ **cup soy sauce**

1½ **teaspoons ground mustard**

½ **teaspoon FRANKS® REDHOT® Original Cayenne Pepper Sauce**

⅛ **teaspoon garlic powder**

1 **tablespoon vegetable oil**

6 **pork chops, ½ to ¾ inch thick**

Preheat oven to 350°F. In 12×8-inch baking dish, layer *half* the potatoes and ⅔ *cup* French Fried Onions. Top with mushrooms and remaining potatoes. In small saucepan, melt butter; stir in soy sauce, mustard, cayenne pepper sauce and garlic powder. Brush *half* soy sauce mixture over potatoes. In large skillet, heat oil. Brown pork chops on both sides; drain. Arrange chops over potatoes and brush with remaining soy sauce mixture. Bake, covered, at 350°F for 1 hour. Bake, uncovered, 15 minutes or until pork chops and potatoes are done. Top chops with remaining ⅔ *cup* onions; bake, uncovered, 5 minutes or until onions are golden brown.   *Makes 4 to 6 servings*

New-Fashioned Spam™ Scalloped Potatoes

Nonstick cooking spray
1 (10¾-ounce) can 99% fat-free
    condensed cream of mushroom soup
½ cup skim milk
1 (2-ounce) jar diced pimiento, drained
¼ teaspoon black pepper
1 (12-ounce) can SPAM® Lite Luncheon
    Meat, cubed
1 cup chopped onion
½ cup frozen peas
4½ cups thinly sliced, peeled potatoes
2 tablespoons dry bread crumbs
1 tablespoon chopped fresh parsley

Preheat oven to 350°F. Spray 2-quart casserole with nonstick cooking spray. In medium bowl, combine soup, milk, pimiento and pepper. In casserole, layer half of each of SPAM®, onion, peas, potatoes and sauce. Repeat layers. Cover. Bake 1 hour or until potatoes are nearly tender. Combine bread crumbs and parsley; sprinkle over casserole. Bake, uncovered, 15 minutes longer or until potatoes are tender. Let stand 10 minutes before serving.   *Makes 6 servings*

Creamy Spam™ Broccoli Casserole

Nonstick cooking spray
1 (7-ounce) package elbow macaroni
2 cups frozen cut broccoli, thawed and
    drained
1 (12-ounce) can SPAM® Lite Luncheon
    Meat, cubed
½ cup chopped red bell pepper
2 cups skim milk
2 tablespoons cornstarch
¼ teaspoon black pepper
1 cup (4 ounces) shredded fat-free
    Cheddar cheese
¾ cup soft bread crumbs
2 teaspoons margarine, melted

Preheat oven to 350°F. Spray 2-quart casserole with
nonstick cooking spray. Cook macaroni according to
package directions; drain. In prepared casserole,
combine macaroni, broccoli, SPAM® and bell pepper. In
small saucepan, stir together milk, cornstarch and
black pepper until cornstarch is dissolved. Bring to a
boil, stirring constantly, until thickened. Reduce heat
to low. Add cheese; stir until melted. Stir sauce into
SPAM™ mixture. Combine bread crumbs and
margarine; sprinkle on top of casserole. Bake
40 minutes or until thoroughly heated.

Makes 8 servings

Ham & Macaroni Twists

- 2 **cups rotini or elbow macaroni, cooked in unsalted water and drained**
- 1⅓ **cups (8 ounces) cubed cooked ham**
- 1⅓ **cups (2.8 ounce can) FRENCH'S® French Fried Onions, divided**
- 1 **package (10 ounces) frozen broccoli spears,* thawed and drained**
- 1 **cup milk**
- 1 **can (10¾ ounces) condensed cream of celery soup**
- 1 **cup (4 ounces) shredded Cheddar cheese, divided**
- ¼ **teaspoon garlic powder**
- ¼ **teaspoon pepper**

Preheat oven to 350°F. In 12×8-inch baking dish, combine hot macaroni, ham and ⅔ *cup* French Fried Onions. Divide broccoli spears into 6 small bunches. Arrange bunches of spears down center of dish, alternating direction of flowerets. In small bowl, combine milk, soup, ½ *cup* cheese and seasonings; pour over casserole. Bake, covered, at 350°F for 30 minutes or until heated through. Top with remaining ½ *cup* cheese and sprinkle ⅔ *cup* onions down center; bake, uncovered, 5 minutes or until onions are golden brown.   *Makes 4 to 6 servings*

*1 small head fresh broccoli (about ½ pound) may be substituted for frozen spears. Divide into spears and cook 3 to 4 minutes before using.

Baked Rigatoni with Sausage

½ pound Italian sausage*
2 cups low fat milk
2 tablespoons all-purpose flour
½ pound rigatoni pasta, cooked and
    drained
2½ cups (10 ounces) grated mozzarella
    cheese
¼ cup grated Parmesan cheese
1 teaspoon LAWRY'S® Garlic Salt
¾ teaspoon LAWRY'S® Seasoned Pepper
2 to 3 tablespoons dry bread crumbs *or*
    ¾ cup croutons

In large skillet, crumble Italian sausage. Brown
5 minutes; drain fat. Stir in mixture of milk and flour;
bring to a boil, stirring constantly. Stir in pasta,
cheeses, Garlic Salt and Seasoned Pepper. Place in
1½-quart baking dish. Bake in 350°F oven 25 minutes.
Sprinkle with bread crumbs; place under broiler to
brown.   *Makes 6 servings*

*¼ pound cooked, diced ham can replace sausage.

Pizza Pasta

1 medium green bell pepper, chopped
1 medium onion, chopped
1 cup sliced mushrooms
½ teaspoon LAWRY'S® Garlic Powder with
  Parsley or Garlic Salt
1 tablespoon vegetable oil
1¾ cups water
1 can (6 ounces) tomato paste
¼ cup sliced ripe olives
1 package (1.5 ounces) LAWRY'S®
  Original-Style Spaghetti Sauce
  Spices & Seasonings
10 ounces mostaccioli, cooked and drained
3 ounces thinly sliced pepperoni
¾ cup shredded mozzarella cheese

In large skillet, sauté bell pepper, onion, mushrooms
and Garlic Powder with Parsley in vegetable oil until
vegetables are tender. Stir in water, tomato paste,
olives and Spaghetti Sauce Spices & Seasonings; blend
well. Bring sauce to a boil; reduce heat. Simmer,
uncovered, 10 minutes. Add mostaccioli and pepperoni;
blend well. Pour into 12×8-inch casserole; top with
cheese. Bake at 350°F 15 minutes or until cheese is
melted.   *Makes 6 servings*

Rigatoni

2 pounds BOB EVANS FARMS® Italian
     Dinner Link Sausage
2 medium onions, sliced
3 green bell peppers, seeded and sliced
3 red bell peppers, seeded and sliced
3 cloves garlic, minced
1 tablespoon sugar
1 teaspoon dried oregano leaves
1 teaspoon dried basil leaves
1 teaspoon dried thyme leaves
   Salt and black pepper to taste
1 (32-ounce) can crushed Italian plum
     tomatoes, undrained
1 pound rigatoni pasta, cooked according
     to package directions and drained
   Chopped fresh parsley (optional)

Cut sausage into 1-inch pieces. Cook in large saucepan
over medium-high heat until well browned. Remove
sausage to paper towels; set aside. Drain off all but
¼ cup drippings. Add all remaining ingredients except
tomatoes, pasta and parsley to drippings. Cook and stir
until vegetables are tender. Stir in reserved sausage
and tomatoes with juice. Bring to a boil. Reduce heat
to low; simmer 15 minutes. Serve over hot pasta.
Garnish with chopped parsley, if desired. Refrigerate
leftovers.   *Makes 8 to 10 servings*

Spaghetti Bake

1 **pound BOB EVANS FARMS® Dinner Link Sausage (regular or Italian)**
1 **(8-ounce) can tomato sauce**
1 **(6-ounce) can tomato paste**
1 **(4-ounce) can sliced mushrooms, drained**
½ **teaspoon salt**
½ **teaspoon dried basil leaves**
½ **teaspoon dried oregano leaves**
6 **ounces spaghetti, cooked according to package directions and drained**
⅓ **cup shredded mozzarella cheese**
2 **tablespoons grated Parmesan cheese Fresh basil leaves and tomato slices (optional)**

Preheat oven to 375°F. Cut sausage links into bite-size pieces. Cook in medium skillet over medium heat until browned, stirring occasionally. Drain off any drippings; set aside. Combine tomato sauce, tomato paste, mushrooms, salt, dried basil and oregano in large bowl. Add spaghetti and reserved sausage; mix well. Spoon into lightly greased 1½-quart casserole dish; sprinkle with cheeses. Bake 20 to 30 minutes or until heated through. Garnish with fresh basil and tomato slices, if desired. Serve hot. Refrigerate leftovers.

Makes 4 servings

Sausage Tetrazzini

1 pound BOB EVANS FARMS® Italian
   Roll Sausage
1 medium onion, chopped
1 red or green bell pepper, chopped
½ pound spaghetti, cooked according to
   package directions and drained
1 (10½-ounce) can condensed cream of
   mushroom soup
1 (10-ounce) can condensed tomato soup
1 (16-ounce) can stewed tomatoes,
   undrained
½ pound fresh mushrooms, chopped
1 teaspoon minced garlic
½ teaspoon black pepper
   Salt to taste
1½ cups (6 ounces) shredded Cheddar
   cheese

Preheat oven to 350°F. Crumble sausage into large
skillet. Cook over medium heat until lightly browned,
stirring occasionally. Remove sausage; set aside. Add
onion and bell pepper to drippings in skillet; cook and
stir until tender. Place in large bowl. Stir in spaghetti,
soups, tomatoes with juice, mushrooms, garlic, black
pepper, salt and reserved sausage; place in 3-quart
casserole dish. Sprinkle with cheese; bake, uncovered,
30 to 35 minutes or until heated through. Serve hot.
Refrigerate leftovers.   *Makes 6 to 8 servings*

Sausage and Feta Strata

8 ounces dried medium pasta shells, cooked, drained
1 pound mild Italian sausage
1 cup sliced green onions (about 6)
¾ cup water
⅔ cup (6-ounce can) CONTADINA® Dalla Casa Buitoni Italian Paste with Roasted Garlic
⅔ cup dry red wine
½ teaspoon dried rosemary, crushed
1½ cups (8 ounces) crumbled feta cheese, divided
2 cups (2 large) sliced zucchini

COOK sausage in large skillet over medium-high heat for 6 to 8 minutes or until no longer pink. Remove from skillet; slice into 2-inch pieces.

ADD green onions to skillet; cook for 2 to 3 minutes. Stir in water, tomato paste, wine and rosemary; bring to a boil. Reduce heat to low; cook for 5 minutes or until flavors are blended.

LAYER half of pasta, half of sauce, *¾ cup* cheese and zucchini in 8-inch-square baking dish. Top with layers of remaining pasta, remaining sauce and *remaining* cheese. Arrange sausage on top.

BAKE, covered, in preheated 350°F. oven for 35 to 40 minutes or until bubbly.   *Makes 4 to 6 servings*

Italian Sausage Supper

1   pound mild Italian sausage
1   cup (1 small) chopped onion
1½   cups (2 small) sliced zucchini
3   cups cooked long-grain white rice
2   cups (17-ounce can) CONTADINA®
       Dalla Casa Buitoni Country Italian
       Cooking Sauce with Mushrooms &
       Roasted Garlic
1   cup (4 ounces) shredded mozzarella
       cheese
¼   cup (1 ounce) grated Romano cheese

CRUMBLE sausage into large skillet. Add onion; cook over medium-high heat for 2 to 3 minutes or until sausage is no longer pink. Drain. Spoon into 2-quart casserole dish. Add zucchini to skillet; cook for 5 minutes or until crisp-tender. Remove from heat.

ADD rice and cooking sauce to sausage; stir. Top with zucchini; sprinkle with mozzarella cheese and Romano cheese.

BAKE, covered, in preheated 350°F. oven for 20 minutes or until heated through.

Makes 6 servings

Smokehouse Red Bean and Sausage Casserole

3 cups chopped onions
3 bacon slices, diced
1 pound smoked sausage, cut into ¼-inch slices
2 cans (15¼ ounces each) kidney beans, undrained
1 medium-sized green bell pepper, chopped
1 cup chopped fresh parsley
1 can (8 ounces) tomato sauce
1 tablespoon LAWRY'S® Seasoned Salt
1 tablespoon Worcestershire sauce
¾ teaspoon hot pepper sauce
½ teaspoon LAWRY'S® Garlic Powder with Parsley
3 cups hot cooked white rice

In Dutch oven or large saucepan, sauté onion and bacon until bacon is just crisp and onion is transparent; drain fat. Add remaining ingredients except rice; blend well. Bring to a boil. Reduce heat to low; simmer, uncovered, 20 minutes, stirring occasionally. Serve with rice.   *Makes 8 servings*

Rice & Sausage Casserole

1   **cup uncooked rice**
1   **pound BOB EVANS FARMS® Zesty Hot
      or Special Seasonings Roll Sausage**
2   **tablespoons butter or margarine**
1   **cup chopped celery**
1   **large onion, chopped**
¼   **cup *each* chopped red and green bell
      peppers**
1   **(10¾-ounce) can condensed cream of
      mushroom soup**
1   **cup milk**
      Salt and black pepper to taste
½   **cup (2 ounces) shredded longhorn or
      Colby cheese**

Cook rice according to package directions; transfer to
large bowl. Preheat oven to 350°F. Crumble sausage
into medium skillet. Cook over medium heat until
lightly browned, stirring occasionally. Remove sausage
to paper towels; set aside. Drain off any drippings and
wipe skillet clean with paper towels. Stir sausage into
cooked rice. Melt butter in same skillet over medium-
high heat until hot. Add celery, onion and bell peppers;
cook and stir until tender. Stir into rice and sausage
mixture. Stir in soup, milk, salt and black pepper; mix
well. Spoon mixture into lightly greased 2-quart
baking dish. Sprinkle with cheese. Bake, uncovered,
40 minutes or until heated through. Serve hot.
Refrigerate leftovers.   *Makes 6 servings*

Quick Cassoulet

2 slices bacon, cut into ½-inch pieces
¾ pound boneless pork chops, sliced
    crosswise ¼ inch thick
1 medium onion, chopped
1 clove garlic, minced
1 teaspoon dried thyme, crushed
1 can (14½ ounces) DEL MONTE®
    FreshCut™ Diced Tomatoes with
    Garlic & Onion Original Recipe
    Stewed Tomatoes
½ cup dry white wine
1 can (15 ounces) white or pinto beans,
    drained

1. Cook bacon in large skillet over medium-high heat until almost crisp.

2. Stir in meat, onion, garlic and thyme. Season with salt and pepper, if desired.

3. Cook 4 minutes. Add tomatoes and wine; bring to boil.

4. Cook, uncovered, over medium-high heat 10 minutes or until thickened, adding beans during last 5 minutes. *Makes 4 servings*

Santa Fe Taco Stew

1 tablespoon vegetable oil
½ cup diced onion
½ teaspoon LAWRY'S® Garlic Powder with
   Parsley
1 can (28 ounces) diced tomatoes,
   undrained
1 can (15 ounces) pinto beans, drained
1 can (8¾ ounces) whole kernel corn,
   drained
1 can (4 ounces) diced green chiles,
   drained
1 package (1 ounce) LAWRY'S® Taco
   Spices & Seasonings
1 cup beef broth
½ teaspoon cornstarch
1 pound pork butt or beef chuck, cooked
   and shredded
   Dairy sour cream (garnish)
   Tortilla chips (garnish)

In Dutch oven or large saucepan, heat oil. Add onion
and Garlic Powder with Parsley; sauté 2 to 3 minutes
until onions are translucent and tender. Add tomatoes
and juice, beans, corn, chiles and Taco Spices &
Seasonings; blend well. In small bowl, gradually blend
broth into cornstarch. Stir into stew. Stir in meat.
Bring to a boil, stirring frequently. Reduce heat to low;
simmer, uncovered, 30 minutes or until desired
consistency, stirring occasionally. Garnish, if desired.
                                        Makes 8 servings

Variation: Substitute 3 cups cooked, shredded chicken
for pork or beef.

Black Bean & Pork Stew

2 (15-ounce) cans cooked black beans, rinsed and drained
2 cups water
1 pound boneless ham, cut into ¾-inch cubes
¾ pound BOB EVANS FARMS® Italian Dinner Link Sausage, cut into 1-inch pieces
¾ pound BOB EVANS FARMS® Smoked Sausage, cut into 1-inch pieces
1 pint cherry tomatoes, stems removed
1 medium onion, chopped
6 cloves garlic, minced
1 teaspoon red pepper flakes
⅛ teaspoon grated orange peel

Preheat oven to 350°F. Combine all ingredients in large Dutch oven. Bring to a boil over high heat, skimming foam off if necessary. Cover; transfer to oven. Bake 30 minutes; uncover and bake 30 minutes more, stirring occasionally. Serve hot or cool slightly, then cover and refrigerate overnight. Remove any fat from surface. Reheat over low heat. Refrigerate leftovers.

Makes 8 servings

Mexican Skillet Rice

¾ pound lean ground pork or lean ground
    beef
1 medium onion, chopped
1 tablespoon plus 1½ teaspoons chili
    powder
1 teaspoon ground cumin
½ teaspoon salt
3 cups cooked brown rice
1 can (16 ounces) pinto beans, drained
2 cans (4 ounces each) diced green
    chiles, undrained
1 medium tomato, seeded and chopped
    (optional)

Brown meat in large skillet over medium-high heat,
stirring to crumble; drain. Return meat to skillet. Add
onion, chili powder, cumin and salt; cook until onion is
soft but not brown. Stir in rice, beans and chiles; heat
thoroughly. Top with tomato, if desired.

Makes 6 servings

Microwave: Combine meat and onion in 2- to
3-quart microwavable dish; stir well. Cover with waxed
paper. Microwave on HIGH 4 to 5 minutes or until
meat is no longer pink, stirring after 2 minutes. Drain.
Add chili powder, cumin, salt, rice, beans and chiles.
Microwave on HIGH 4 to 5 minutes or until
thoroughly heated, stirring after 2 minutes. Top with
tomato.

Favorite recipe from **USA Rice Council**

Country Skillet Hash

2 **tablespoons butter or margarine**
4 **pork chops (¾ inch thick), diced**
¼ **teaspoon black pepper**
¼ **teaspoon cayenne pepper (optional)**
1 **medium onion, chopped**
2 **cloves garlic, minced**
1 **can (14½ ounces) DEL MONTE®**
    FreshCut™ **Whole New Potatoes,**
    drained and diced
1 **can (14½ ounces) DEL MONTE®**
    FreshCut™ **Diced Tomatoes,**
    undrained
1 **medium green bell pepper, chopped**
½ **teaspoon thyme, crushed**

1. Melt butter over medium heat in large skillet. Add meat; cook, stirring occasionally, until no longer pink in center. Season with black pepper and cayenne pepper, if desired.

2. Add onion and garlic; cook until tender. Stir in potatoes, tomatoes, green pepper and thyme. Cook 5 minutes, stirring frequently. Season with salt, if desired.   *Makes 4 servings*

Tip: The hash may be topped with a poached or fried egg.

Southwest Pork and Dressing

1 pound boneless pork, cut into 1-inch
   strips
2 teaspoons chili powder
¼ cup margarine or butter
½ cup diagonally sliced green onions
1½ cups water
1 cup frozen sweet corn, thawed
1 can (4 ounces) chopped green chilies,
   drained
3 cups STOVE TOP® Cornbread Stuffing
   Mix in the Canister
1¼ cups (5 ounces) KRAFT® Natural
   Shredded Monterey Jack Cheese,
   divided

TOSS meat with chili powder. Melt margarine in large skillet over medium-high heat. Add meat and onions; cook and stir until meat is browned.

STIR in water, corn and chilies. Bring to boil. Stir in stuffing mix and ¾ cup of the cheese. Remove from heat. Sprinkle with remaining ½ cup cheese. Cover. Let stand 5 minutes. *Makes 4 to 6 servings*

Sweet & Sour Mustard Pork

1   pound boneless pork, cut into strips
¼   cup GREY POUPON® Dijon Mustard,
      divided
3   teaspoons soy sauce, divided
1   (3-ounce) package chicken-flavored
      Ramen noodles
1   (8-ounce) can pineapple chunks,
      drained, reserving juice
½   cup water
2   tablespoons firmly packed light brown
      sugar
1   tablespoon cornstarch
½   teaspoon grated fresh ginger
2   cups broccoli flowerets
½   cup chopped red or green cabbage
½   cup chopped red bell pepper
½   cup coarsely chopped onion
2   tablespoons vegetable oil

In medium bowl, combine pork strips, 2 tablespoons mustard and 1 teaspoon soy sauce. Refrigerate for 1 hour.

In small bowl, combine remaining 2 tablespoons mustard and 2 teaspoons soy sauce, chicken flavor packet from noodles, reserved pineapple juice, water, brown sugar, cornstarch and ginger; set aside. Cook Ramen noodles according to package directions; drain and set aside.

In large skillet, over medium-high heat, stir-fry vegetables in oil until tender-crisp; remove from skillet. Add pork mixture; stir-fry for 3 to 4 minutes or until done. Return vegetables to skillet with pineapple chunks and cornstarch mixture; heat until mixture thickens and begins to boil. Add cooked noodles, tossing to coat well. Garnish as desired. Serve immediately.   *Makes 4 servings*

Sausage Ham Jambalaya

6 ounces spicy smoked sausage links,
   sliced
6 ounces cooked ham, diced
2 cans (14½ ounces each) DEL MONTE®
   FreshCut™ Diced Tomatoes with
   Green Pepper & Onion
1 cup uncooked long-grain white rice
1 large clove garlic, minced
1 tablespoon chopped fresh parsley
1 bay leaf

Brown sausage and ham in heavy 4-quart saucepan.
Drain tomatoes, reserving liquid; pour liquid into
measuring cup. Add water to measure 1½ cups. Add
reserved liquid, tomatoes and remaining ingredients to
sausage mixture. Cover and simmer 30 to 35 minutes,
stirring occasionally. Remove and discard bay leaf.
Garnish with additional chopped parsley, if desired.

Makes 4 to 6 servings

Fiesta Pork Chops

4 well-trimmed ¾-inch-thick pork chops
2 teaspoons chili powder
1 tablespoon vegetable oil
1 package (6.8 ounces) RICE-A-RONI
     Spanish Rice
2 tablespoons margarine or butter
1 can (14½ ounces) tomatoes, undrained
     and chopped
½ cup chopped green bell pepper *or* 1 can
     (4 ounces) chopped green chiles,
     drained
½ cup chopped onion

1. Evenly sprinkle both sides of pork chops with chili powder. In large skillet, brown pork chops in oil over medium-high heat. Drain; set aside.

2. In same skillet, combine rice-vermicelli mix and margarine. Sauté over medium heat, stirring frequently until vermicelli is golden brown.

3. Stir in 1¾ cups water, contents of seasoning packet, tomatoes, green pepper and onion; bring to a boil over high heat.

4. Place pork chops over rice mixture; return to a boil. Cover; reduce heat. Simmer 25 to 30 minutes or until liquid is absorbed and rice and chops are tender.

Makes 4 servings

Honey Nut Stir-Fry

1 pound pork steak or loin or boneless chicken breast
¾ cup orange juice
⅓ cup honey
3 tablespoons soy sauce
1 tablespoon cornstarch
¼ teaspoon ground ginger
2 tablespoons vegetable oil, divided
2 large carrots, sliced diagonally
2 stalks celery, sliced diagonally
½ cup cashews or peanuts
Hot cooked rice

Cut pork into thin strips; set aside. Combine orange juice, honey, soy sauce, cornstarch and ginger in small bowl; mix well. Heat 1 tablespoon oil in large skillet over medium-high heat. Add carrots and celery; stir-fry about 3 minutes. Remove vegetables; set aside. Pour remaining 1 tablespoon oil into skillet. Add meat; stir-fry about 3 minutes. Return vegetables to skillet; add sauce mixture and nuts. Cook and stir over medium-high heat until sauce comes to a boil and thickens. Serve over rice. *Makes 4 to 6 servings*

Favorite recipe from **National Honey Board**

Mandarin Pork Stir-Fry

1½ cups DOLE® Mandarin Tangerine Juice
or Pineapple Orange Juice, divided
Vegetable cooking spray
12 ounces lean pork tenderloin or
boneless, skinless chicken breast
halves, cut into thin strips
1 tablespoon finely chopped fresh ginger
or ½ teaspoon ground ginger
2 cups DOLE® Shredded Carrots
½ cup chopped DOLE® Pitted Prunes
4 DOLE® Green Onions, diagonally cut
into 1-inch pieces
2 tablespoons low-sodium soy sauce
1 teaspoon cornstarch
Hot cooked rice (optional)

• **Heat** 2 tablespoons juice over medium-high heat in large, nonstick skillet sprayed with cooking spray until juice bubbles.

• **Add** pork and ginger. Cook and stir 3 minutes or until pork is no longer pink; remove pork from skillet.

• **Heat** 3 tablespoons juice in skillet. Add carrots, prunes and green onions; cook and stir 3 minutes.

• **Stir** soy sauce and cornstarch into remaining juice; add to carrot mixture in skillet. Return pork to skillet; cover. Cook 2 minutes or until heated through and sauce is slightly thickened. Serve over rice and garnish with green onions and orange peel, if desired.

Makes 4 servings

 Seafaring

SUPPERS

Baked Fish with Potatoes and Onions

1   pound baking potatoes, very thinly
        sliced
1   large onion, very thinly sliced
1   small red bell pepper, thinly sliced
      Salt
      Black pepper
½   teaspoon dried oregano leaves, divided
1   pound lean fish fillets, cut 1 inch thick
¼   cup butter or margarine
¼   cup all-purpose flour
2   cups milk
¾   cup (3 ounces) shredded Cheddar
        cheese

Preheat oven to 375°F.

Arrange ½ of the potatoes in buttered 3-quart casserole.
Top with ½ *each* of the onion and bell pepper. Season
with salt and black pepper. Sprinkle with ¼ teaspoon
oregano. Arrange fish in 1 layer over vegetables.
Arrange remaining potatoes, onion and bell pepper
over fish. Season with salt, black pepper and remaining
¼ teaspoon oregano.

Melt butter in medium saucepan over medium heat.
Stir in flour; cook until bubbly, stirring constantly.
Gradually stir in milk. Cook until thickened, stirring
constantly. Pour white sauce over casserole. Cover and
bake 40 minutes or until potatoes are tender. Sprinkle
with cheese. Bake, uncovered, about 5 minutes more
or until cheese is melted.   *Makes 4 servings*

Superb Fillet of Sole & Vegetables

1   can (10¾ ounces) condensed cream of
    celery soup
½   cup milk
1   cup (4 ounces) shredded Swiss cheese,
    divided
½   teaspoon dried basil, crumbled
¼   teaspoon seasoned salt
¼   teaspoon pepper
1   package (10 ounces) frozen baby
    carrots, thawed and drained
1   package (10 ounces) frozen asparagus
    cuts, thawed and drained
1⅓ cups (2.8 ounce can) FRENCH'S®
    French Fried Onions, divided
1   pound unbreaded sole fillets, thawed if
    frozen

Preheat oven to 375°F. In small bowl, combine soup,
milk, *½ cup* cheese and the seasonings; set aside. In
12×8-inch baking dish, combine carrots, asparagus
and *⅔ cup* French Fried Onions. Roll up fish fillets. (If
fillets are wide, fold in half lengthwise before rolling.)
Place fish rolls upright along center of vegetable
mixture. Pour soup mixture over fish and vegetables.
Bake, covered, at 375°F for 30 minutes or until fish
flakes easily with fork. Stir vegetables; top fish with
remaining *½ cup* cheese and *⅔ cup* onions. Bake,
uncovered, 3 minutes or until onions are golden
brown.   *Makes 3 to 4 servings*

So-Easy Fish Divan

1 package (about 1⅛ ounces) cheese
   sauce mix
1⅓ cups milk
1 bag (16 ounces) frozen vegetable
   combination (Brussels sprouts,
   carrots, cauliflower), thawed and
   drained
1⅓ cup (2.8 ounce can) FRENCH'S®
   French Fried Onions, divided
1 pound unbreaded fish fillets, thawed if
   frozen
½ cup (2 ounces) shredded Cheddar
   cheese

Preheat oven to 375°F. In small saucepan, prepare
cheese sauce mix according to package directions
using 1⅓ cups milk. In 12×8-inch baking dish,
combine vegetables and ⅔ cup French Fried Onions;
top with fish fillets. Pour cheese sauce over fish and
vegetables. Bake, covered, at 375°F for 25 minutes or
until fish flakes easily with fork. Top fish with Cheddar
cheese and remaining ⅔ *cup* onions; bake, uncovered,
3 minutes or until onions are golden brown.

Makes 3 to 4 servings

Fish Broccoli Casserole

1 **package (10 ounces) frozen broccoli spears, thawed and drained**
1 **cup cooked, flaked whitefish**
1 **can (10¾ ounces) condensed cream of mushroom soup**
½ **cup milk**
¼ **teaspoon salt**
⅛ **teaspoon freshly ground black pepper**
½ **cup crushed potato chips**

Preheat oven to 425°F. Grease 1½-quart casserole. Layer broccoli in prepared casserole. Combine fish, soup, milk, salt and pepper in large bowl.

Spread fish mixture over broccoli. Sprinkle with potato chips. Bake 12 to 15 minutes or until golden brown.

Makes 4 servings

Favorite recipe from **Florida Department of Agriculture & Consumer Services, Bureau of Seafood and Aquaculture**

Spicy Snapper & Black Beans

1½ pounds fresh red snapper fillets, cut
     into 4 portions (6 ounces each)
     Juice of 1 lime
½   teaspoon coarsely ground black pepper
     Nonstick cooking spray
1   cup GUILTLESS GOURMET® Spicy
     Black Bean Dip
½   cup water
½   cup (about 35) crushed GUILTLESS
     GOURMET® Baked Tortilla Chips
     (yellow or white corn)
1   cup GUILTLESS GOURMET® Salsa
     (mild, medium or hot)

Wash fish thoroughly; pat dry with paper towels. Place
fish in 13×9-inch glass baking dish. Pour juice over
top; sprinkle with pepper. Cover and refrigerate 1 hour.

Preheat oven to 350°F. Coat 11×7-inch glass baking
dish with cooking spray. Combine bean dip and water
in small bowl; spread 1 cup bean mixture in bottom of
prepared baking dish. Place fish over bean mixture,
discarding juice. Spread remaining bean mixture over
top of fish; sprinkle with crushed chips.

Bake about 20 minutes or until chips are lightly browned
and fish turns opaque and flakes easily when tested with
fork. Serve fish with salsa.   *Makes 4 servings*

Note: This recipe can be made with 4 boneless skinless
chicken breast halves in place of red snapper fillets.
Prepare as directed and bake about 40 minutes or until
chicken is no longer pink in center. Serve as directed.

Tuna & Asparagus au Gratin

1   **pound fresh asparagus**
¼   **cup water**
¼   **cup butter or margarine**
3   **tablespoons all-purpose flour**
¼   **teaspoon salt**
⅛   **teaspoon pepper**
¾   **cup low-fat milk**
¼   **cup dry white wine**
1   **can (12 ounces) STARKIST® Tuna,**
     drained and broken into chunks
3   **tablespoons seasoned bread crumbs**
3   **tablespoons grated Parmesan**

Trim asparagus; place in microwavable dish with tips toward center. Add water. Cover; micro-cook on High power 5 minutes, or until tender; rotate dish once.

In a 1-quart microwavable bowl micro-cook ½ of the butter on High power for 30 seconds, or until melted. Stir in flour, salt and pepper. Blend in milk and wine. Micro-cook on High power for 4 to 6 minutes, or until mixture thickens; stir every 2 minutes. Stir in tuna. Pour into 4 microwavable ramekins. Drain asparagus; arrange over tuna mixture. Melt remaining butter in microwavable dish on High power for 30 seconds. Drizzle over tops. Sprinkle with bread crumbs and cheese. Micro-cook on High power for 3 to 5 minutes, or until heated; rotate once.   *Makes 4 servings*

Surfin' Tuna Casserole

3   eggs
¾   cup milk
2   cups STOVE TOP® Stuffing Mix for
      Chicken in the Canister
1½ cups (6 ounces) KRAFT® Natural
      Shredded Colby/Monterey Jack
      Cheese, divided
1   cup frozen green peas, thawed
1   can (6 ounces) tuna, drained, flaked
½   cup condensed cream of mushroom
      soup
½   cup chopped green onions
2   tablespoons chopped pimiento

BEAT eggs in large bowl; stir in milk. Stir in stuffing
mix, 1 cup of the cheese, peas, tuna, soup, onions and
pimiento until well mixed. Spoon into greased 9-inch
microwavable pie plate. Cover loosely with wax paper.

MICROWAVE on HIGH 5 minutes. Stir thoroughly to
completely mix center and outside edges; smooth top.
Cover.

MICROWAVE 5 minutes or until center is no longer
wet. Sprinkle with remaining ½ cup cheese; cover. Let
stand 5 minutes.   *Makes 6 servings*

Tuna Tortilla Roll-Ups

1 can (10¾ ounces) condensed cream of
celery soup
1 cup milk
1 can (9 ounces) tuna, drained and flaked
1 package (10 ounces) frozen broccoli
spears, thawed, drained and cut into
1-inch pieces
1 cup (4 ounces) shredded Cheddar
cheese, divided
1⅓ cups (2.8 ounce can) FRENCH'S®
French Fried Onions, divided
6 (7-inch) flour or corn tortillas
1 medium tomato, chopped

Preheat oven to 350°F. In small bowl, combine soup
and milk; set aside. In medium bowl, combine tuna,
broccoli, ½ cup cheese and ⅔ cup French Fried Onions;
stir in ¾ cup soup mixture. Divide tuna mixture evenly
among tortillas; roll up tortillas. Place, seam-side
down, in lightly greased 13×9-inch baking dish. Stir
tomato into remaining soup mixture; pour down
center of roll-ups. Bake, covered, at 350°F for 35
minutes or until heated through. Top center of roll-ups
with remaining ½ cup cheese and ⅔ cup onions; bake,
uncovered, 5 minutes or until onions are golden
brown.   *Makes 6 servings*

Tag-Along Tuna Bake

 3 to 4 tablespoons butter or margarine,
     softened
12 slices bread
 1 can (12 ounces) water-packed tuna,
     drained and flaked
 1 cup chopped celery
1⅓ cups (2.8 ounce can) FRENCH'S®
     French Fried Onions
 2 cups milk
 1 cup mayonnaise
 4 eggs, slightly beaten
 1 can (10¾ ounces) condensed cream of
     mushroom soup
 3 slices (¾ ounce each) process American
     cheese, cut diagonally into halves

Butter 1 side of each bread slice; arrange 6 slices
buttered-side down in 13×9-inch baking dish. Layer
tuna, celery and ⅔ *cup* French Fried Onions evenly
over bread. Top with remaining bread slices, buttered-
side down. In medium bowl, combine milk,
mayonnaise, eggs and soup; mix well. Pour evenly over
layers in baking dish; cover and refrigerate overnight.
Bake, covered, at 350°F for 30 minutes. Uncover and
bake 15 minutes or until center is set. Arrange cheese
slices down center of casserole, overlapping slightly,
points all in same direction. Top with remaining ⅔ *cup*
onions; bake, uncovered, 5 minutes or until onions are
golden brown.   *Makes 8 servings*

Crab and Corn Enchilada Casserole

Spicy Tomato Sauce (page 233),
divided
10 to 12 ounces fresh crabmeat or flaked
or chopped surimi crab
1 package (10 ounces) frozen corn,
thawed and drained
1½ cups (6 ounces) shredded reduced-fat
Monterey Jack cheese, divided
1 can (4 ounces) diced mild green chilies
12 (6-inch) corn tortillas
1 lime, cut into 6 wedges
Low-fat sour cream (optional)

1. Preheat oven to 350°F. Prepare Spicy Tomato Sauce.

2. Combine 2 cups Spicy Tomato Sauce, crab, corn,
1 cup cheese and chilies in medium bowl.

3. Cut each tortilla into 4 wedges. Place one third of
tortilla wedges in bottom of shallow 3- to 4-quart
casserole, overlapping to make solid layer. Spread half
of crab mixture on top. Repeat with another layer of
tortilla wedges, remaining crab mixture and remaining
tortillas. Spread remaining 1 cup Spicy Tomato Sauce
over top; cover.

4. Bake 30 to 40 minutes or until heated through.
Sprinkle with remaining ½ cup cheese and bake
uncovered 5 minutes or until cheese melts. Squeeze
lime over individual servings. Serve with low-fat sour
cream, if desired.   *Makes 6 servings*

Spicy Tomato Sauce

2 cans (15 ounces each) no-salt-added
  stewed tomatoes, undrained *or*
  6 medium tomatoes
2 teaspoons olive oil
1 medium onion, chopped
1 tablespoon minced garlic
2 tablespoons chili powder
2 teaspoons ground cumin
2 teaspoons dried oregano leaves, crushed
1 teaspoon ground cinnamon
¼ teaspoon crushed red pepper
¼ teaspoon ground cloves

1. Place tomatoes with liquid in food processor or blender; process until finely chopped. Set aside.

2. Heat oil over medium-high heat in large saucepan or Dutch oven. Add onion and garlic. Cook and stir 5 minutes or until onion is tender. Add chili powder, cumin, oregano, cinnamon, red pepper and cloves. Cook and stir 1 minute.

3. Add tomatoes; reduce heat to medium-low. Simmer, uncovered, 20 minutes or until sauce is reduced to 3 to 3¼ cups.   *Makes about 3 cups*

Company Crab

- 1 **pound blue crabmeat, fresh, frozen or pasteurized**
- 1 **can (15 ounces) artichoke hearts, drained**
- 1 **can (4 ounces) sliced mushrooms, drained**
- 2 **tablespoons butter or margarine**
- 2½ **tablespoons all-purpose flour**
- ½ **teaspoon salt**
- ⅛ **teaspoon ground red pepper**
- 1 **cup half-and-half**
- 2 **tablespoons dry sherry**
- 2 **tablespoons crushed corn flakes**
- 1 **tablespoon grated Parmesan cheese Paprika**

Preheat oven to 450°F. Thaw crabmeat if frozen. Remove any pieces of shell or cartilage. Cut artichoke hearts in half; place artichokes in well-greased, shallow 1½-quart casserole. Add crabmeat and mushrooms; cover and set aside.

Melt butter in small saucepan over medium heat. Stir in flour, salt and ground red pepper. Gradually stir in half-and-half. Continue cooking until sauce thickens, stirring constantly. Stir in sherry. Pour sauce over crabmeat. Combine corn flakes and cheese in small bowl; sprinkle over casserole. Sprinkle with paprika. Bake 12 to 15 minutes or until bubbly.

Makes 6 servings

Favorite recipe from **Florida Department of Agriculture and Consumer Services, Bureau of Seafood and Aquaculture**

Tuna and Broccoli Bake

1   package (16 ounces) frozen broccoli
cuts, thawed and well drained
2   slices bread, cut in ½-inch cubes
1   can (12 ounces) STARKIST® Solid
White or Chunk Light Tuna, drained
and chunked
2   cups cottage cheese
1   cup shredded Cheddar cheese
3   eggs
¼   teaspoon ground black pepper

Place broccoli on bottom of 2-quart baking dish. Top
with bread cubes and tuna. In medium bowl, combine
cottage cheese, Cheddar cheese, eggs and pepper.
Spread evenly over tuna mixture. Bake in 400°F oven
30 minutes or until golden brown and puffed.

Makes 4 servings

Salmon Linguini Supper

8 ounces linguini, cooked in unsalted
    water and drained
1 package (10 ounces) frozen peas
1 cup milk
1 can (10¾ ounces) condensed cream of
    celery soup
¼ cup (1 ounce) grated Parmesan cheese
⅛ teaspoon dried tarragon, crumbled
    (optional)
1 can (15½ ounces) salmon, drained and
    flaked
1⅓ cups (2.8 ounce can) FRENCH'S®
    French Fried Onions, divided
1 egg, slightly beaten
¼ teaspoon salt
¼ teaspoon pepper

Preheat oven to 375°F. Return hot pasta to saucepan;
stir in peas, milk, soup, cheese and tarragon; spoon
into 12×8-inch baking dish. In medium bowl, using
fork, combine salmon, ⅔ *cup* French Fried Onions,
egg, salt and pepper. Shape salmon mixture into
4 oval patties. Place patties on pasta mixture. Bake,
covered, at 375°F for 40 minutes or until patties are
done. Top patties with remaining ⅔ *cup* onions; bake,
uncovered, 3 minutes or until onions are golden
brown.   *Makes 4 servings*

Microwave Directions: Prepare pasta mixture as above,
except increase milk to 1¼ cups; spoon into 12×8-inch
microwave-safe dish. Cook, covered, on HIGH 3
minutes; stir. Prepare salmon patties as above using

2 eggs. Place patties on pasta mixture. Cook, covered, 10 to 12 minutes or until patties are done, rotating dish halfway through cooking time. Top patties with remaining onions; cook, uncovered, 1 minute. Let stand 5 minutes.

Sole Almondine

1   **package (6.5 ounces) RICE-A-RONI®**
    Broccoli Au Gratin
1   **medium zucchini**
4   **sole, scrod or orange roughy fillets**
1   **tablespoon lemon juice**
¼   **cup grated Parmesan cheese**
    Salt and pepper (optional)
¼   **cup sliced almonds**
2   **tablespoons margarine or butter, melted**

1. Prepare Rice-A-Roni® mix as package directs.

2. While Rice-A-Roni® is simmering, cut zucchini lengthwise into 12 thin slices. Heat oven to 350°F.

3. In 11×7-inch glass baking dish, spread prepared rice evenly. Set aside. Sprinkle fish with lemon juice, 2 tablespoons cheese, salt and pepper, if desired. Place zucchini strips over fish; roll up. Place fish seam-side down on rice.

4. Combine almonds and margarine; sprinkle evenly over fish. Top with remaining 2 tablespoons cheese. Bake 20 to 25 minutes or until fish flakes easily with fork.   *Makes 4 servings*

Spinach-Noodle Casserole

1 package (10 ounces) frozen chopped
   spinach
2 cups low-fat ricotta cheese
¼ cup reduced-calorie mayonnaise or
   salad dressing
1 egg
2 teaspoons dried chives
1 teaspoon dried basil, crushed
½ teaspoon dill weed
¼ teaspoon salt
⅛ teaspoon pepper
4 ounces wide egg noodles or fusilli,
   cooked and drained
1 can (9¼ ounces) STARKIST® Tuna,
   drained and broken into chunks
½ cup shredded low-fat mozzarella cheese

Place opened spinach package in a shallow
microwavable bowl. Micro-cook, uncovered, on High
power for 4 to 6 minutes, or until thawed, turning
every 2 minutes. Let stand for 2 minutes. Drain well
and squeeze out excess moisture. In a blender
container or food processor bowl combine spinach,
ricotta, mayonnaise, egg and seasonings. Cover and
process until smooth. In a 9×9×2-inch microwavable
casserole spread noodles. Top with tuna, then spread
cheese mixture over tuna to edge of dish. Cover loosely;
micro-cook on High power for 8 to 11 minutes, or until
mixture is hot in center. Sprinkle mozzarella cheese
over top. Let stand, covered, for 5 minutes, or until
cheese is melted. *Makes 4 servings*

Shrimp Noodle Supreme

 1 **package (8 ounces) spinach noodles,
     cooked and drained**
 1 **package (3 ounces) cream cheese,
     cubed and softened**
1½ **pounds medium shrimp, peeled and
     deveined**
 ½ **cup butter, softened
     Salt and pepper to taste**
 1 **can (10¾ ounces) condensed cream of
     mushroom soup**
 1 **cup sour cream**
 ½ **cup half-and-half**
 ½ **cup mayonnaise**
 1 **tablespoon chopped chives**
 1 **tablespoon chopped parsley**
 ½ **teaspoon Dijon mustard**
 ¾ **cup (3 ounces) shredded sharp Cheddar
     cheese**

Preheat oven to 325°F. Combine noodles and cream
cheese in medium bowl. Spread noodle mixture into
bottom of greased 13×9-inch glass casserole. Cook
shrimp in butter in large skillet over medium-high
heat until pink and tender, about 5 minutes. Season
with salt and pepper. Spread shrimp over noodles.

Combine soup, sour cream, half-and-half, mayonnaise,
chives, parsley and mustard in another medium bowl.
Spread over shrimp. Sprinkle Cheddar cheese over top.
Bake 25 minutes or until hot and cheese is melted.

Makes 6 servings

Shrimp in Angel Hair Pasta Casserole

- 1 cup half-and-half
- 1 cup plain yogurt
- 2 eggs, beaten
- ½ cup (2 ounces) shredded Swiss cheese
- ⅓ cup crumbled feta cheese
- ⅓ cup chopped fresh parsley
- ¼ cup chopped fresh basil *or* 1 teaspoon dried basil leaves
- 1 teaspoon dried oregano leaves
- 1 package (9 ounces) fresh angel hair pasta, uncooked
- 1 jar (16 ounces) mild, thick and chunky salsa
- 1 pound medium shrimp, peeled and deveined
- ½ cup (2 ounces) shredded Monterey Jack cheese

Preheat oven to 350°F. Grease 12×8-inch baking dish. Combine half-and-half, yogurt, eggs, Swiss cheese, feta cheese, parsley, basil and oregano in medium bowl; mix well. Place half the pasta in bottom of prepared pan. Cover with salsa. Add half the shrimp. Cover with remaining pasta. Spread egg mixture over pasta and top with remaining shrimp. Sprinkle with Monterey Jack cheese. Bake 30 minutes or until bubbly. Let stand 10 minutes. *Makes 6 servings*

Favorite recipe from **Southeast United Dairy Industry Association, Inc.**

Foolproof Clam Fettucine

1 package (6 ounces) fettucine-style
   noodles with creamy cheese sauce
   mix
¾ cup milk
1 can (6½ ounces) chopped clams,
   undrained
¼ cup (1 ounce) grated Parmesan cheese
1 can (4 ounces) mushroom stems and
   pieces, drained
1⅓ cups (2.8 ounce can) FRENCH'S®
   French Fried Onions, divided
2 tablespoons diced pimiento
1 teaspoon parsley flakes

Preheat oven to 375°F. In large saucepan, cook noodles
according to package directions; drain. Return hot
noodles to saucepan; stir in sauce mix, milk, undrained
clams, Parmesan cheese, mushrooms, ⅔ *cup* French
Fried Onions, pimiento and parsley flakes. Heat and
stir 3 minutes or until bubbly. Pour into 10×6-inch
baking dish. Bake, covered, at 375°F for 30 minutes or
until thickened. Place remaining ⅔ *cup* onions around
edges of casserole; bake, uncovered, 3 minutes or until
onions are golden brown.   *Makes 4 servings*

Microwave Directions: Prepare noodle mixture as
above; pour into 10×6-inch microwave-safe dish.
Cook, covered, on HIGH 4 to 6 minutes or until heated
through, stirring noodle mixture halfway through
cooking time. Top with remaining onions as above;
cook, uncovered, 1 minute. Let stand 5 minutes.

Herb-Baked Fish & Rice

1½ cups hot chicken broth
½ cup uncooked long-grain white rice
¼ teaspoon Italian seasoning
¼ teaspoon garlic powder
1 package (10 ounces) frozen chopped broccoli, thawed and drained
1⅓ cups (2.8 ounce can) FRENCH'S® French Fried Onions, divided
1 tablespoon grated Parmesan cheese
1 pound unbreaded fish fillets, thawed if frozen
 Paprika (optional)
½ cup (2 ounces) shredded Cheddar cheese

Preheat oven to 375°F. In 12×8-inch baking dish, combine hot broth, uncooked rice and seasonings. Bake, covered, at 375°F for 10 minutes. Top with broccoli, ⅔ *cup* French Fried Onions and the Parmesan cheese. Place fish fillets diagonally down center of dish; sprinkle fish lightly with paprika. Bake, covered, at 375°F for 20 to 25 minutes or until fish flakes easily with fork. Stir rice. Top fish with Cheddar cheese and remaining ⅔ *cup* onions; bake, uncovered, 3 minutes or until onions are golden brown.

Makes 3 to 4 servings

Microwave Directions: In 12×8-inch microwave-safe dish, prepare rice mixture as above, except reduce broth to 1¼ cups. Cook, covered, on HIGH 5 minutes, stirring halfway through cooking time. Stir in broccoli, ½ *can* onions and the Parmesan cheese. Arrange fish fillets in single layer on top of rice mixture; sprinkle fish lightly with paprika. Cook, covered, on MEDIUM (50-60%) 18 to 20 minutes or until fish flakes easily with fork and rice is done, rotating dish halfway through cooking time. Top fish with Cheddar cheese and remaining onions; cook, uncovered, on HIGH 1 minute or until cheese melts. Let stand 5 minutes.

Crab and Brown Rice Casserole

- 1 **pound blue crabmeat, thawed if frozen**
- 3 **eggs, slightly beaten**
- 1 **cup mayonnaise**
- 1 **cup cooked brown rice**
- ¾ **cup evaporated milk**
- ¾ **cup (3 ounces) shredded Cheddar cheese**
- ¼ **teaspoon hot pepper sauce**

Preheat oven to 350°F. Grease 1½-quart casserole; set aside. Remove any pieces of cartilage from crabmeat. Set aside.

Combine eggs, mayonnaise, brown rice, milk, cheese and pepper sauce in large bowl. Stir in crabmeat. Bake 30 to 35 minutes or until knife inserted 1 inch from center comes out clean. *Makes 6 servings*

Favorite recipe from **Florida Department of Agriculture & Consumer Services, Bureau of Seafood and Aquaculture**

Sicilian Fish and Rice Bake

3 tablespoons olive or vegetable oil
¾ cup chopped onion
½ cup (1 large stalk) chopped celery
1 clove garlic, finely chopped
½ cup long-grain white rice
3½ cups (two 14.5-ounce cans)
    CONTADINA® Dalla Casa Buitoni
    Recipe Ready Diced Tomatoes,
    undrained
1 teaspoon salt
1 teaspoon ground black pepper
½ teaspoon granulated sugar
⅛ teaspoon cayenne pepper
1 pound firm fish fillets
¼ cup chopped fresh parsley

HEAT oil in large skillet over medium-high heat. Add onion, celery and garlic; cook for 2 to 3 minutes or until vegetables are tender. Stir in rice; cook for 5 minutes or until rice is slightly browned. Stir in tomatoes and juice, salt, black pepper, sugar and cayenne pepper. Place fish in greased 12×7-inch baking dish; spoon rice mixture over fish.

BAKE, covered, in preheated 400°F. oven for 45 to 50 minutes or until rice is tender. Cool in dish for 5 minutes; sprinkle with parsley.

Makes 6 servings

Tuna-Swiss Pie

2 cups cooked unsalted regular rice
   (⅔ cup uncooked)
1 tablespoon butter or margarine
¼ teaspoon garlic powder
3 eggs
1⅓ cups (2.8 ounce can) FRENCH'S®
   French Fried Onions, divided
1 cup (4 ounces) shredded Swiss cheese,
   divided
1 can (9 ounces) water-packed tuna,
   drained and flaked
1 cup milk
¼ teaspoon salt
¼ teaspoon pepper

Preheat oven to 400°F. To hot rice in saucepan, add
butter, garlic powder and *1 slightly beaten egg;* mix
thoroughly. Spoon rice mixture into *ungreased* 9-inch
pie plate. Press rice mixture firmly onto bottom and up
side of pie plate to form a crust. Layer *⅔ cup* French
Fried Onions, *½ cup* cheese and the tuna evenly over
rice crust. In small bowl, combine milk, remaining
eggs and the seasonings; pour over tuna filling. Bake,
uncovered, at 400°F for 30 to 35 minutes or until
center is set. Top with remaining *½ cup* cheese and *⅔
cup* onions; bake, uncovered, 1 to 3 minutes or until
onions are golden brown.   *Makes 4 to 6 servings*

Homestyle Tuna Pot Pie

1 package (15 ounces) refrigerated pie
     crusts
1 can (12 ounces) STARKIST® Solid
     White or Chunk Light Tuna, drained
     and chunked
1 package (10 ounces) frozen peas and
     carrots, thawed and drained
½ cup chopped onion
1 can (10¾ ounces) cream of potato or
     cream of mushroom soup
⅓ cup milk
½ teaspoon poultry seasoning or dried
     thyme
     Salt and pepper to taste

Line 9-inch pie pan with one crust; set aside. Reserve
second crust. In medium bowl, combine remaining
ingredients; mix well. Pour tuna mixture into pie shell;
top with second crust. Crimp edges to seal. Cut slits in
top crust to vent. Bake in 375°F oven 45 to 50 minutes
or until golden brown.   *Makes 6 servings*

Biscuit-Topped Tuna Bake

2 tablespoons vegetable oil
½ cup chopped onion
½ cup chopped celery
1 can (12 ounces) STARKIST® Solid
   White or Chunk Light Tuna, drained
   and chunked
1 can (10¾ ounces) cream of potato soup
1 package (10 ounces) frozen peas and
   carrots, thawed
¾ cup milk
¼ teaspoon ground black pepper
¼ teaspoon garlic powder
1 can (7½ ounces) refrigerator flaky
   biscuits

In large skillet, heat oil over medium-high heat; sauté onion and celery until onion is soft. Add remaining ingredients except biscuits; heat thoroughly. Transfer mixture to 1½-quart casserole. Arrange biscuits around top edge of dish; bake in 400°F oven 10 to 15 minutes or until biscuits are golden brown.

Makes 4 to 6 servings

Easy Three Cheese Tuna Soufflé

    4   cups large croutons*
    2½ cups milk
    4   large eggs
    1   can (10¾ ounces) cream of celery soup
    3   cups shredded cheese—use a
          combination of Cheddar, Monterey
          Jack and Swiss
    1   can (12 ounces) STARKIST® Solid
          White or Chunk Light Tuna, drained
          and flaked
    1   tablespoon butter or margarine
    ½   cup chopped celery
    ½   cup finely chopped onion
    ¼   pound mushrooms, sliced

In bottom of lightly greased 13×9-inch baking dish,
arrange croutons. In medium bowl, beat together milk,
eggs and soup; stir in cheeses and tuna. In small
skillet, melt butter over medium heat. Add celery,
onion and mushrooms; sauté until onion is soft.

Spoon sautéed vegetables over croutons; pour egg-tuna
mixture over top. Cover; refrigerate overnight. Remove
from refrigerator 1 hour before baking; bake in 325°F
oven 45 to 50 minutes or until hot and bubbly.

Makes 8 servings

*Use garlic and herb or ranch-flavored croutons.

Chesapeake Crab Strata

4 tablespoons butter or margarine
4 cups unseasoned croutons
2 cups (8 ounces) shredded Cheddar
   cheese
2 cups milk
8 eggs, beaten
½ teaspoon dry mustard
½ teaspoon seafood seasoning
   Salt and black pepper to taste
1 pound crabmeat, picked over to remove
   any shells

Preheat oven to 325°F. Place butter in 11×7-inch
baking dish. Heat in oven until melted; tilt to coat dish.
Remove dish from oven; spread croutons over melted
butter. Top with cheese; set aside.

Combine milk, eggs, dry mustard, seafood seasoning,
salt and black pepper; mix well. Pour egg mixture over
cheese in dish; sprinkle with crabmeat. Bake for 50
minutes or until mixture is set. Remove from oven. Let
stand for about 10 minutes.

Makes 6 to 8 servings

Zesty Cioppino

2 tablespoons olive oil
1¼ cups (1 medium) chopped onion
1 cup (2 large stalks) chopped celery
½ cup chopped green bell pepper
3½ cups (two 14.5-ounce cans)
   CONTADINA® Dalla Casa Buitoni
   Recipe Ready Diced Tomatoes,
   undrained
2 cups water
¾ cup dry red wine or chicken broth
⅔ cup (6-ounce can) CONTADINA® Dalla
   Casa Buitoni Italian Paste with
   Roasted Garlic
1 teaspoon Italian herb seasoning
½ teaspoon salt
½ teaspoon ground black pepper
1 pound fresh clams in shells
1 pound firm white fish, cut into pieces
1 pound uncooked bay scallops or
   shrimp, peeled and deveined

HEAT oil in large saucepan over medium-high heat. Add onion, celery and bell pepper; cook for 3 to 4 minutes or until tender.

STIR in tomatoes and juice, water, wine, tomato paste, Italian herb seasoning, salt and pepper. Bring to a boil. Reduce heat to low; cook, covered, for 20 minutes.

ADD clams and fish; cook for 5 minutes. Add shrimp; cook for 5 to 10 minutes or until shrimp turn pink and clams are opened. *Makes 6 to 8 servings*

Tortilla Soup with Grouper

1 tablespoon vegetable oil
1 small onion, chopped
2 small cloves garlic, minced
3½ cups chicken broth
1½ cups tomato juice
1 cup chopped tomatoes
1 can (4 ounces) diced green chilies,
   drained
2 teaspoons Worcestershire sauce
1 teaspoon ground cumin
1 teaspoon chili powder
1 teaspoon salt
⅛ teaspoon black pepper
3 corn tortillas, cut into 1-inch strips
1 cup corn
1 pound grouper fillets, washed, patted
   dry and cut into 1-inch cubes
   Fresh parsley sprigs and jalapeño
   pepper rings for garnish

Heat oil in large saucepan over medium-high heat. Add onion and garlic; cook until softened. Stir in broth, tomato juice, tomatoes, chilies, Worcestershire sauce, cumin, chili powder, salt and pepper. Bring soup to a boil; cover and simmer 10 minutes. Add tortillas and corn to broth mixture; cover and simmer 8 to 10 minutes.

Stir in grouper. Do not cover. Continue to simmer until fish is opaque and flakes easily when tested with fork. Serve immediately.   *Makes 6 servings*

Fisherman's Stew

2 cups water
1 pound fish fillets (scrod, halibut,
    monkfish or cod), cut into 2-inch
    pieces
1 clove garlic, minced
1 tablespoon FILIPPO BERIO® Olive Oil
1 medium onion, chopped
¼ cup chopped almonds
¼ cup seasoned dry bread crumbs
2 cups vegetable broth or bouillon
2 medium tomatoes, diced
¼ teaspoon paprika
¼ teaspoon freshly ground black pepper
    Salt

In large saucepan or Dutch oven, bring water to a boil
over high heat. Add fish and garlic. Cover; reduce heat
to low and simmer 15 minutes or until fish is opaque
and flakes easily when tested with fork. Remove fish
with slotted spoon; set aside. Reserve stock (about
2 cups).

Meanwhile, in small nonstick skillet, heat olive oil over
medium heat until hot. Add onion; cook and stir
5 minutes or until softened. Add almonds and bread
crumbs; cook and stir 3 to 5 minutes or until lightly
browned. Add to reserved fish stock along with
vegetable broth, tomatoes, paprika and pepper. Add
fish; cover and cook until fish is heated through.
Season to taste with salt. Serve hot.

Makes 4 to 6 servings

Spicy Shrimp Gumbo

½ cup vegetable oil
½ cup all-purpose flour
1 cup chopped onion
½ cup chopped fresh parsley
½ cup chopped celery
½ cup sliced green onions
6 cloves garlic, minced
4 cups chicken broth or water*
1 package (10 ounces) frozen sliced okra,
    thawed (optional)
1 teaspoon salt
½ teaspoon ground red pepper
2 pounds medium shrimp, peeled and
    deveined
3 cups hot cooked rice

Blend oil and flour in large heavy stockpot. Cook over medium-high heat 10 to 15 minutes or until roux is dark brown, stirring often. Add onion, parsley, celery, green onions and garlic to roux. Cook over medium-high heat 5 to 10 minutes or until vegetables are tender. Add broth, okra, salt and red pepper. Cover; simmer 15 minutes. Add shrimp; simmer 3 to 5 minutes or until shrimp turn pink and opaque. Place about ⅓ cup rice into each wide-rimmed soup bowl; top with gumbo. *Makes 8 servings*

*Traditional gumbo's thickness is like stew. If you prefer it thinner, add 1 to 2 cups additional broth.

Southern Italian Clam Chowder

2 slices (2 ounces) bacon, chopped
1 cup (1 small) chopped onion
½ cup chopped carrot
½ cup chopped celery
3½ cups (two 14.5-ounce cans)
   CONTADINA® Dalla Casa Buitoni
   Recipe Ready Diced Tomatoes,
   undrained
1 cup (8-ounce can) CONTADINA® Dalla
   Casa Buitoni Tomato Sauce
1 cup (8-ounce bottle) clam juice
½ teaspoon chopped fresh rosemary
⅛ teaspoon ground black pepper
1½ cups (two 6½-ounce cans) chopped
   clams, undrained

COOK bacon in large saucepan over medium-high heat for 1 minute. Add onion, carrot and celery; cook for 2 to 3 minutes. Stir in tomatoes and juice, tomato sauce, clam juice, rosemary and pepper.

BRING to a boil. Reduce heat to low; cook for 15 minutes. Stir in clams and juice; cook for 5 minutes or until heated through.   *Makes 6 servings*

Paella

1 tablespoon olive oil
½ pound chicken breast cubes
1 cup uncooked long-grain rice*
1 medium onion, chopped
1 clove garlic, minced
1½ cups chicken broth*
1 can (8 ounces) stewed tomatoes,
      chopped, reserving liquid
½ teaspoon paprika
⅛ to ¼ teaspoon ground red pepper
⅛ teaspoon ground saffron
½ pound medium shrimp, peeled and
      deveined
1 small red pepper, cut into strips
1 small green pepper, cut into strips
½ cup frozen green peas

Heat oil in Dutch oven over medium-high heat until
hot. Add chicken; cook, stirring occasionally, until
browned. Add rice, onion, and garlic. Cook, stirring
occasionally, until onion is tender and rice is lightly
browned. Add broth, tomatoes, tomato liquid, paprika,
ground red pepper, and saffron. Bring to a boil; stir.
Reduce heat; cover and simmer 10 minutes. Add
shrimp, pepper strips, and peas. Cover and simmer
10 minutes or until rice is tender and liquid is
absorbed.   *Makes 6 servings*

*If using medium-grain rice, use 1¼ cups of broth; if using parboiled
rice, use 1¾ cups of broth.

Favorite recipe from **USA Rice Council**

Cajun Catfish Skillet

 2 cups water
 1 cup uncooked long-grain rice
 ¼ teaspoon salt
 ¼ teaspoon ground red pepper
 ¼ teaspoon ground white pepper
 ¼ teaspoon ground black pepper
 ½ cup minced green onions
 ½ cup minced green pepper
 ½ cup minced celery
 2 cloves garlic, minced
 1 tablespoon margarine
 1 pound catfish nuggets or other firm
       flesh white fish
 1 can (15½ ounces) tomato sauce
 1 teaspoon dried oregano leaves

Combine water, rice, salt, red pepper, white pepper and
black pepper in 3-quart saucepan. Bring to a boil; stir.
Reduce heat; cover and simmer 15 minutes or until
rice is tender and liquid is absorbed. Cook onions,
green pepper, celery and garlic in margarine in large
skillet over medium-high heat until tender. Stir
vegetable mixture, catfish nuggets, tomato sauce and
oregano into hot rice. Cover and cook over medium
heat 7 to 8 minutes or until catfish flakes with fork.

Makes 4 servings

To microwave: Combine water, rice, salt, red pepper,
white pepper and black pepper in deep 2½- to 3-quart
microwavable baking dish. Cover and cook on HIGH
5 minutes. Reduce setting to MEDIUM (50% power)

and cook 15 minutes or until rice is tender and liquid is absorbed. Combine onions, green pepper, celery, garlic and margarine in 2-cup glass measure; cook on HIGH 2 minutes or until onions are tender. Stir vegetable mixture, catfish nuggets, tomato sauce and oregano into hot rice. Cover and cook on HIGH 6 to 8 minutes, stirring after 3 minutes, or until catfish flakes with fork.

Favorite recipe from USA Rice Council

Tuna and Rice Skillet Dinner

  1   package (6½ ounces) chicken flavored
        rice mix
  ½   cup chopped onion
        Water
 1½ cups frozen peas and carrots, thawed
  1   can (10¾ ounces) cream of mushroom
        soup
  ⅛   teaspoon ground black pepper
  1   can (12 ounces) STARKIST® Solid
        White or Chunk Light Tuna, drained
        and chunked
  ⅓   cup toasted slivered almonds (optional)

In medium saucepan, combine rice mix and onion. Add water and prepare rice according to package directions. Stir in vegetables, soup and pepper; blend well. Simmer, covered, 5 to 7 minutes, stirring occasionally. Stir in tuna; top with almonds, if desired.

Makes 4 to 6 servings

Tuna with Broccoli and Cheddar

3 cups low-fat milk

1 envelope (1.8 ounces) white sauce mix

2 teaspoons chicken bouillon granules

1½ cups shredded Cheddar cheese

3 cups cooked chopped broccoli

½ teaspoon finely ground black pepper

¼ to ½ teaspoon grated lemon peel

1 can (12 ounces) STARKIST® Solid White or Chunk Light Tuna, drained and chunked

2 small (8 ounces each) round French bread loaves, hollowed out and heated*

In 1½-quart saucepan, combine milk, white sauce mix and bouillon granules, using wire whisk to blend. Cook over medium-high heat, whisking constantly until bouillon dissolves and sauce has thickened slightly. Reduce heat; add cheese, stirring until melted. Stir in broccoli, pepper and lemon peel; heat thoroughly. Add tuna just before serving. Divide mixture between hollowed loaves. Cut into wedges.

Makes 6 servings

*Brush French bread with garlic butter before heating.

Angel Hair Al Fresco

¾ cup skim milk
1 tablespoon margarine or butter
1 package (4.8 ounces) PASTA RONI®
        Angel Hair Pasta with Herbs
1 can (6 ounces) white tuna in water,
        drained, flaked, *or* 1½ cups chopped
        cooked chicken
2 medium tomatoes, chopped
⅓ cup sliced green onions
¼ cup dry white wine or water
¼ cup slivered almonds, toasted (optional)
1 tablespoon chopped fresh basil *or*
        1 teaspoon dried basil

1. In 3-quart saucepan, combine 1⅓ cups water, skim milk and margarine. Bring just to a boil.

2. Stir in pasta, contents of seasoning packet, tuna, tomatoes, onions, wine, almonds and basil. Return to a boil; reduce heat to medium.

3. Boil, uncovered, stirring frequently, 6 to 8 minutes. Sauce will be thin, but will thicken upon standing.

4. Let stand 3 minutes or until desired consistency. Stir before serving.   *Makes 4 servings*

Tuna and Pasta Frittata

1 tablespoon olive oil
2 cups cooked spaghetti
4 large eggs
2 tablespoons milk
¼ cup prepared pesto sauce
1 can (6 ounces) STARKIST® Solid
   White or Chunk Light Tuna, drained
   and flaked
½ cup shredded mozzarella cheese

Preheat broiler. In medium ovenproof skillet, heat oil over medium-high heat; sauté spaghetti. In bowl, combine eggs, milk and pesto sauce; blend well. Add tuna; pour mixture over hot spaghetti. Cook over medium-low heat, stirring occasionally, until eggs are almost completely set. Sprinkle cheese over cooked eggs; place under broiler until cheese is bubbly and golden. Serve hot or at room temperature.

Makes 2 to 4 servings

Bacon-Tuna Parmesano

½ cup milk
2 tablespoons margarine or butter
1 package (4.8 ounces) PASTA RONI®
  Parmesano
1 package (10 ounces) frozen peas
1 can (6 ounces) white tuna in water,
  drained, flaked
4 slices crisply cooked bacon, crumbled
½ cup sliced green onions

1. In round 3-quart microwaveable glass casserole, combine 1⅔ cups water, milk and margarine. Microwave, uncovered, on HIGH 4 to 5 minutes or until boiling.

2. Stir in pasta, contents of seasoning packet, frozen peas, tuna, bacon and onions.

3. Microwave, uncovered, on HIGH 9 to 10 minutes or until peas are tender, stirring after 3 minutes.

4. Cover; let stand 3 to 4 minutes. Sauce will thicken upon standing. Stir before serving.

Makes 4 servings

Pad Thai (Thai Fried Noodles)

7¼ cups water, divided
12 ounces dried thin rice stick noodles*
 4 tablespoons vegetable oil, divided
 ¼ cup soy sauce
 3 tablespoons brown sugar
 2 tablespoons lime juice
 1 tablespoon anchovy paste
 2 eggs, lightly beaten
12 ounces medium shrimp, peeled and
    deveined
 2 cloves garlic, minced
 1 tablespoon paprika
 ¼ to ½ teaspoon crushed red pepper
 1 cup canned bean sprouts, rinsed and
    drained, divided
 ½ cup coarsely chopped unsalted dry
    roasted peanuts
 4 green onions with tops, cut into 1-inch
    pieces

1. Place 6 cups water in wok; bring to a boil over high heat. Add noodles; cook 2 minutes or until tender but still firm, stirring frequently. Drain; rinse under cold running water to stop cooking. Drain again and place noodles in large bowl. Add 1 tablespoon oil and toss lightly to coat; set aside.

2. Combine remaining 1¼ cups water, soy sauce, brown sugar, juice and anchovy paste in small bowl; set aside.

3. Heat wok over medium heat 2 minutes or until hot. Drizzle 1 tablespoon oil into wok and heat 30 seconds. Add eggs; stir-fry 1 minute or just until set on bottom. Turn eggs over; stir to scramble. Remove to medium bowl. Increase heat to high.

4. Drizzle 1 tablespoon oil into wok and heat 30 seconds. Add shrimp and garlic; stir-fry 2 minutes or until shrimp begin to turn pink and opaque. Remove shrimp to bowl with eggs. Reduce heat to medium.

5. Drizzle remaining 1 tablespoon oil into wok and heat 15 seconds. Stir in paprika and red pepper to taste. Add noodles and anchovy mixture; cook and stir about 5 minutes or until noodles are softened. Stir in ¾ cup bean sprouts. Add peanuts and onions; toss and cook about 1 minute or until onions are tender. Add eggs and shrimp; stir-fry until heated through. Transfer to serving plate; top with remaining bean sprouts.

Makes 4 servings

*If rice stick noodles are unavailable, use fine egg noodles, thin spaghetti, vermicelli or angel hair pasta.

Lemon-Garlic Shrimp

1   package (6.2 ounces) RICE-A-RONI®
    With ⅓ Less Salt Broccoli Au Gratin
1   tablespoon margarine or butter
1   pound raw medium shrimp, shelled and
    deveined or large scallops, halved
1   medium red or green bell pepper, cut
    into short thin strips
2   cloves garlic, minced
½   teaspoon Italian seasoning
½   cup reduced-sodium or regular chicken
    broth
1   tablespoon lemon juice
1   tablespoon cornstarch
3   medium green onions, cut into ½-inch
    pieces
1   teaspoon grated lemon peel

1. Prepare Rice-A-Roni® mix as package directs.

2. While Rice-A-Roni® is simmering, heat margarine in second large skillet or wok over medium-high heat. Add shrimp, red pepper, garlic and Italian seasoning. Stir-fry 3 to 4 minutes or until seafood is opaque.

3. Combine chicken broth, lemon juice and cornstarch, mixing until smooth. Add broth mixture and onions to skillet. Stir-fry 2 to 3 minutes or until sauce thickens.

4. Stir ½ teaspoon lemon peel into rice. Serve rice topped with shrimp mixture; sprinkle with remaining ½ teaspoon lemon peel.   *Makes 4 servings*

Shrimp à la Louisiana

1 tablespoon margarine
1½ cups uncooked long-grain white rice
1 medium onion, chopped
1 green pepper, chopped
2¾ cups beef broth
¼ teaspoon salt
¼ teaspoon ground black pepper
¼ teaspoon hot pepper sauce
1 pound medium shrimp, peeled and
   deveined
1 can (4 ounces) sliced mushrooms,
   drained
3 tablespoons snipped parsley
¼ cup sliced green onions for garnish
   (optional)

Melt margarine in 3-quart saucepan. Add rice, onion
and green pepper. Cook 2 to 3 minutes. Add broth, salt,
black pepper and pepper sauce; bring to a boil. Cover
and simmer 15 minutes. Add shrimp, mushrooms and
parsley. Cook 5 minutes longer or until shrimp turn
pink. Garnish with green onions.   *Makes 8 servings*

Favorite recipe from **USA Rice Council**

Shrimp Classico

⅔ cup milk
2 tablespoons margarine or butter
1 package (4.8 ounces) PASTA RONI®
    Angel Hair Pasta with Herbs
1 clove garlic, minced
1 package (10 ounces) frozen chopped
    spinach, thawed, well drained
1 package (10 ounces) frozen precooked
    shrimp, thawed, well drained
1 jar (2 ounces) chopped pimento,
    drained

1. In 3-quart round microwaveable glass casserole, combine 1⅔ cups water, milk and margarine. Microwave, uncovered, on HIGH 4 to 5 minutes or until boiling.

2. Gradually add pasta while stirring. Separate pasta with a fork, if needed. Stir in contents of seasoning packet and garlic.

3. Microwave, uncovered, on HIGH 4 minutes, stirring gently after 2 minutes. Separate pasta with a fork, if needed. Stir in spinach, shrimp and pimento. Microwave on HIGH 1 to 2 minutes. Sauce will be very thin, but will thicken upon standing.

4. Let stand, uncovered, 2 minutes or until desired consistency. Stir before serving.

Makes 4 servings

Shrimp Curry

1¼ pounds raw large shrimp
1 large onion, chopped
½ cup canned light coconut milk
3 cloves garlic, minced
2 tablespoons finely chopped fresh ginger
2 to 3 teaspoons hot curry powder
¼ teaspoon salt
1 can (14½ ounces) diced tomatoes
1 teaspoon cornstarch
2 tablespoons chopped fresh cilantro
3 cups hot cooked rice

1. Peel shrimp, leaving tails attached and reserving shells. Place shells in large saucepan; cover with water. Bring to a boil over high heat. Reduce heat to low; simmer 15 to 20 minutes. Strain shrimp stock and set aside. Discard shells.

2. Spray large skillet with nonstick cooking spray; heat over medium heat. Add onion; cover and cook 5 minutes. Add ½ cup shrimp stock, coconut milk, garlic, ginger, curry powder and salt; bring to a boil. Reduce heat to low and simmer 10 to 15 minutes or until onion is tender.

3. Add shrimp and tomatoes to skillet; return mixture to a simmer. Cook 3 minutes.

4. Stir cornstarch into 1 tablespoon cooled shrimp stock until dissolved. Add mixture to skillet with cilantro; simmer 1 to 2 minutes or just until slightly thickened, stirring occasionally. Serve over rice.

Makes 6 servings

Meatless

MAGIC

Italian Eggplant Parmigiana

1   large eggplant, sliced ¼ inch thick
2   eggs, beaten
½   cup dry bread crumbs
1   can (14½ ounces) DEL MONTE®
      FreshCut™ Diced Tomatoes with
      Green Pepper & Onion Italian Recipe
      Stewed Tomatoes
1   can (15 ounces) DEL MONTE® Tomato
      Sauce
2   cloves garlic, minced
½   teaspoon dried basil
6   ounces mozzarella cheese, sliced

1. Dip eggplant slices into eggs, then bread crumbs; arrange in single layer on baking sheet. Broil 4 inches from heat until brown and tender, about 5 minutes per side. *Reduce oven temperature to 350°F.*

2. Place eggplant in 13×9-inch baking dish. Combine tomatoes, tomato sauce, garlic and basil; pour over eggplant and top with cheese.

3. Cover and bake at 350°F for 30 minutes or until heated through. Sprinkle with grated Parmesan cheese, if desired.   *Makes 4 servings*

Double Spinach Bake

8   ounces uncooked spinach fettuccine
     noodles
1   cup fresh mushroom slices
1   green onion with top, finely chopped
1   clove garlic, minced
4   to 5 cups fresh spinach, coarsely
     chopped *or* 1 package (10 ounces)
     frozen spinach, thawed and drained
1   tablespoon water
1   container (15 ounces) nonfat ricotta
     cheese
¼   cup skim milk
1   egg
½   teaspoon ground nutmeg
½   teaspoon ground black pepper
¼   cup (1 ounce) shredded reduced-fat
     Swiss cheese

1. Preheat oven to 350°F. Cook pasta according to package directions, omitting salt. Drain; set aside.

2. Spray medium skillet with nonstick cooking spray. Add mushrooms, green onion and garlic. Cook and stir over medium heat until mushrooms are softened. Add spinach and water. Cover; cook until spinach is wilted, about 3 minutes.

3. Combine ricotta cheese, milk, egg, nutmeg and black pepper in large bowl. Gently stir in noodles and vegetables; toss to coat evenly.

4. Lightly coat shallow 1½-quart casserole with nonstick cooking spray. Spread noodle mixture in casserole. Sprinkle with Swiss cheese.

5. Bake 25 to 30 minutes or until knife inserted halfway into center comes out clean.

Makes 6 servings

Eggplant Pasta Bake

4	ounces bow-tie pasta
1	pound eggplant, diced
1	clove garlic, minced
¼	cup olive oil
1½	cups shredded Monterey Jack cheese
1	cup sliced green onions
½	cup grated Parmesan cheese
1	can (14½ ounces) DEL MONTE® *FreshCut*™ Diced Tomatoes with Basil, Garlic & Oregano

1. Preheat oven to 350°F. Cook pasta according to package directions; drain.

2. Cook eggplant and garlic in oil in large skillet over medium-high heat until tender. Toss eggplant with cooked pasta, 1 cup Monterey Jack cheese, green onions and Parmesan cheese.

3. Place in greased 9-inch square baking dish. Top with tomatoes and remaining ½ cup Monterey Jack cheese. Bake 15 minutes or until heated through.

Makes 6 servings

Wisconsin Swiss Linguine Tart

½ cup butter, divided
2 garlic cloves, minced
30 thin French bread slices
3 tablespoons flour
1 teaspoon salt
¼ teaspoon white pepper
Dash nutmeg
2½ cups milk
¼ cup grated Wisconsin Parmesan cheese
2 eggs, beaten
2 cups (8 ounces) shredded Wisconsin
Baby Swiss cheese, divided
8 ounces fresh linguine, cooked, drained
⅓ cup green onion slices
2 teaspoons dried basil, crushed
2 plum tomatoes

Melt ¼ cup butter. Add garlic; cook 1 minute. Brush 10-inch pie plate with butter mixture; line bottom and sides with bread, allowing bread to come 1 inch over sides. Brush bread with remaining butter mixture. Bake at 350°F for 5 minutes or until lightly browned. Set aside.

Melt remaining butter in saucepan over low heat. Blend in flour and seasonings. Gradually add milk; cook, stirring constantly, until thickened. Remove from heat; add Parmesan cheese. Stir small amount of sauce into eggs; mix well. Stir in remaining sauce.

Toss 1¼ cups Swiss cheese with linguine, green onion and basil. Pour sauce over linguine mixture; mix well. Pour into crust. Cut each tomato lengthwise into eight slices; place on tart. Sprinkle with remaining ¾ cup cheese. Bake at 350°F for 25 minutes or until warm. Let stand 5 minutes.   *Makes 8 servings*

Favorite recipe from **Wisconsin Milk Marketing Board**

Pasta Primavera Casserole

3   **cups uncooked rotini pasta**
1⅓ **cups (2.8 ounce can) FRENCH'S®**
    French Fried Onions, divided
½   **cup zucchini, thinly sliced**
1   **tomato, chopped**
1   **cup frozen peas, thawed**
1   **cup (4 ounces) shredded mozzarella**
    cheese
½   **cup (2 ounces) grated Parmesan cheese**
2   **cups milk**
2   **tablespoons flour**
1   **tablespoon HERB-OX® Instant Chicken**
    Flavor Bouillon

Cook pasta according to package directions; drain. Return pasta to saucepan. Toss lightly with ⅔ *cup* French Fried Onions, vegetables, cheeses, milk, flour and bouillon; mix well. Pour into a 12×8-inch baking dish. Bake, uncovered, at 350°F for 35 minutes or until heated through, stirring halfway through. Top with remaining ⅔ *cup* onions. Bake, uncovered, 5 minutes or until onions are golden.   *Makes 6 servings*

Spaghetti & Egg Casserole

12 ounces uncooked spaghetti
3 tablespoons FILIPPO BERIO® Olive
   Oil
¾ cup sliced onion
4 eggs, beaten
3 tablespoons grated Parmesan cheese
   Additional grated Parmesan cheese
   (optional)
   Additional beaten egg (optional)

Preheat oven to 350°F. Cook pasta according to
package directions until al dente (tender but still firm).
Drain. Meanwhile, in medium skillet, heat olive oil
over medium heat until hot. Add onion; cook and stir
5 minutes or until softened. Remove with slotted spoon
to large bowl. When oil is cool, grease 9-inch square
baking pan with a portion of oil from skillet.

Add 4 beaten eggs and 3 tablespoons Parmesan cheese
to onion; mix well. Add pasta; toss until lightly coated.
Pour into prepared pan. Bake 10 to 20 minutes or until
egg is firm.

Sprinkle with additional Parmesan cheese or brush
with additional beaten egg, if desired. Broil, 4 to 5
inches from heat, until golden brown.

Makes 6 servings

Valley Eggplant Parmigiano

2 **eggplants (about 1 pound each)**
⅓ **cup olive or vegetable oil**
1 **container (15 ounces) ricotta cheese**
2 **packages (1 ounce each) HIDDEN**
      VALLEY RANCH® Milk Recipe
      Original Ranch® Salad Dressing Mix
2 **eggs**
2 **teaspoons dry bread crumbs**
1 **cup tomato sauce**
½ **cup shredded mozzarella cheese**
1 **tablespoon grated Parmesan cheese**
      Chopped parsley

Preheat oven to 350°F. Cut eggplants into ½-inch slices. Brush some of the oil onto two large baking sheets. Arrange eggplant slices in single layer on sheets and brush tops with additional oil. Bake until eggplant is fork-tender, about 20 minutes.

In large bowl, whisk together ricotta cheese and salad dressing mix; whisk in eggs. In 13×9-inch baking dish, layer half the eggplant. Sprinkle 1 teaspoon of the bread crumbs over eggplant; spread all the ricotta mixture on top. Arrange remaining eggplant in another layer. Sprinkle with remaining 1 teaspoon bread crumbs; top with tomato sauce. Sprinkle cheeses on top. Bake until cheeses begin to brown, about 30 minutes. Sprinkle with parsley.

Makes 6 to 8 servings

Eggplant Parmigiana

2 cups plain dry bread crumbs
1 cup (4 ounces) shredded ALPINE
    LACE® Fat Free Pasteurized Process
    Skim Milk Cheese Product—For
    Parmesan Lovers
2 tablespoons Italian seasoning
2 teaspoons minced garlic, divided
2 medium-size unpeeled eggplants
    (2 pounds), cut crosswise into
    ½-inch-thick slices
2 egg whites, lightly beaten
2 tablespoons olive oil, divided
1½ cups thin strips red onion
1 can (28 ounces) crushed tomatoes in
    puree, undrained
⅓ cup water
½ cup slivered fresh basil leaves
1 teaspoon sugar
¼ teaspoon red pepper flakes
¼ teaspoon salt
2 cups (8 ounces) shredded ALPINE
    LACE® Fat Free Pasteurized Process
    Skim Milk Cheese Product—For
    Mozzarella Lovers
¼ cup minced fresh parsley

1. Preheat the oven to 375°F. Spray 2 baking sheets and a 13×9×3-inch baking dish with nonstick cooking spray. In a food processor or blender, process the bread crumbs, Parmesan, Italian seasoning and 1 teaspoon of the garlic for 30 seconds. Spread on a plate.

2. Dip the eggplant slices into the egg whites, coat both sides with the crumb mixture, then arrange in a single layer on the baking sheets. Drizzle with 1 tablespoon of the oil. Bake the eggplant for 40 minutes or until crisp, turning the slices over once. Remove the eggplant from the oven and reduce the temperature to 350°F.

3. While the eggplant bakes, make the sauce: In a large skillet, heat the remaining tablespoon of the oil over medium-high heat. Add the onion and the remaining teaspoon of garlic and sauté for 5 minutes or until soft. Stir in the tomatoes and their puree, the water, basil, sugar, red pepper flakes and salt. Simmer, uncovered, for 5 minutes.

4. In the baking dish, layer a third of the eggplant slices, a third of the sauce and a third of the mozzarella cheese; repeat 2 times. Bake for 30 minutes or until bubbly; sprinkle with the parsley.

Makes 8 servings

Rigatoni with Four Cheeses

3 cups milk
1 tablespoon chopped carrot
1 tablespoon chopped celery
1 tablespoon chopped onion
1 tablespoon fresh parsley sprigs
¼ teaspoon black peppercorns
¼ teaspoon hot pepper sauce
½ bay leaf
   Dash nutmeg
¼ cup Wisconsin butter
¼ cup flour
½ cup (2 ounces) grated Wisconsin
   Parmesan cheese
¼ cup (1 ounce) grated Wisconsin
   Romano cheese
12 ounces rigatoni, cooked, drained
1½ cups (6 ounces) shredded Wisconsin
   Cheddar cheese
1½ cups (6 ounces) shredded Wisconsin
   Mozzarella cheese
¼ teaspoon chili powder

In a 2-quart saucepan, combine first 9 ingredients ending with nutmeg. Bring to a boil. Reduce heat to low; simmer 10 minutes. Strain, reserving liquid. Melt butter in 2-quart saucepan over low heat. Blend in flour. Gradually add reserved liquid; cook, stirring constantly, until thickened. Remove from heat. Add Parmesan and Romano cheeses; stir until blended. Pour over pasta; toss well. Combine Cheddar and Mozzarella cheeses. In buttered 2-quart casserole, layer ½ of pasta mixture, Cheddar cheese mixture and remaining pasta mixture. Sprinkle with chili powder. Bake at 350°F for 25 minutes or until hot.   *Makes 6 servings*

Favorite recipe from **Wisconsin Milk Marketing Board**

Macaroni Italiano

1 tablespoon salt
8 ounces elbow macaroni
2 cups (16 ounces) canned tomatoes,
   undrained
½ teaspoon baking soda
1 cup (8 ounces) canned tomato sauce
1¼ cups low-fat cottage cheese, at room
   temperature
¼ cup grated Parmesan cheese
1 (10-ounce) package frozen chopped
   spinach, thawed and squeezed dry
1½ cups frozen peas, thawed
1 teaspoon dried basil leaves
½ teaspoon pepper
¾ cup chopped toasted* California
   walnuts
2 tablespoons chopped fresh parsley

Preheat oven to 350°F. Bring about 6 quarts of water to a boil with 1 tablespoon salt. Add macaroni and cook, stirring occasionally, for about 8 minutes, or until done.

Meanwhile, place tomatoes and juice into large bowl. Add baking soda; break tomatoes into small chunks. Stir in tomato sauce. Add cheeses, spinach, peas, basil and pepper; toss to combine and set aside. When macaroni is done, drain well. Add to cheese mixture and toss to mix thoroughly; pour mixture into oiled 2½-quart baking dish. Cover baking dish with foil and bake casserole for 20 minutes; uncover and bake 10

minutes more. Stir in walnuts and sprinkle with
parsley.   *Makes 6 servings*

*toasting is optional

Favorite recipe from **Walnut Marketing Board**

Spicy Ravioli and Cheese

- 1 **medium red bell pepper, thinly sliced**
- 1 **medium green bell pepper, thinly sliced**
- 1 **medium yellow bell pepper, thinly sliced**
- 1 **tablespoon olive or vegetable oil**
- ½ **teaspoon LAWRY'S® Seasoned Salt**
- ¼ **teaspoon LAWRY'S® Garlic Powder with Parsley**
- ¼ **teaspoon sugar**
- 1 **package (8 or 9 ounces) fresh or frozen ravioli**
- 1½ **cups chunky salsa, divided**
- 4 **ounces mozzarella cheese, thinly sliced**
- 2 **green onions, sliced**

In broiler-proof baking dish, place bell peppers;
sprinkle with oil, Seasoned Salt, Garlic Powder with
Parsley and sugar. Broil 15 minutes or until tender and
browned, turning once. Prepare ravioli according to
package directions. Pour ¾ cup salsa in bottom of
8-inch square baking dish. Alternate layers of bell
peppers, ravioli, cheese and green onions. Pour
remaining ¾ cup salsa over layers. Cover with foil; bake
in 350°F oven 15 to 20 minutes or until heated
through and cheese melts.   *Makes 4 to 6 servings*

Spinach Ziti Casserole

1 pound ziti or other pasta
2 teaspoons vegetable oil
1 medium onion, chopped
1 (16-ounce) can tomato sauce
1 (10-ounce) package frozen spinach,
    thawed and squeezed dry
2 teaspoons sugar
2 tablespoons dried oregano leaves
½ teaspoon black pepper
½ teaspoon chili powder
1 (16-ounce) container non-fat cottage
    cheese
1 (15-ounce) can kidney beans, drained
    and rinsed

In large saucepan, cook pasta according to directions.
When done, drain pasta and return to saucepan.

Meanwhile, heat oil in a medium saucepan over
medium-high heat. Add onion; cook and stir 5
minutes. Add tomato sauce, spinach, sugar, oregano,
pepper and chili powder. Reduce heat to low; cook
15 minutes. Add sauce to pasta along with cottage
cheese and beans; mix well. Pour into 2-quart baking
dish; cover. Bake in 350°F oven 20 minutes.

Makes 6 servings

Note: If desired, recipe can be finished on the stove top.
Do not remove pasta mixture from saucepan; heat
thoroughly over medium heat, stirring occasionally.

Favorite recipe from **The Sugar Association, Inc.**

Vegetarian Paella

1 tablespoon olive oil
1 medium onion, chopped
1 serrano* pepper, finely chopped
1 red bell pepper, diced
1 green bell pepper, diced
3 cloves garlic, minced
½ teaspoon saffron threads, crushed
½ teaspoon paprika
1 cup uncooked long-grain rice
3 cups water
1 can (15 ounces) chick-peas, rinsed and
   drained
14 ounces artichoke hearts in water,
   drained, cut into halves
1 cup frozen green peas
1½ teaspoons grated lemon peel

1. Preheat oven to 375°F. Heat oil in large paella pan or heavy, ovenproof skillet over medium-high heat. Add onion, serrano pepper and bell peppers; cook and stir about 7 minutes.

2. Add garlic, saffron and paprika; cook 3 minutes. Add rice; cook and stir 1 minute. Add water, chick-peas, artichoke hearts, green peas and lemon peel; mix well.

3. Cover and bake 25 minutes or until rice is tender.

Makes 6 servings

*Chili peppers can sting and irritate the skin; wear rubber gloves when handling peppers and do not touch eyes. Wash hands after handling.

Cheese-Stuffed Peppers

6 small green, yellow or red bell peppers
2 cups canned crushed tomatoes, undrained
⅓ cup water
⅓ cup slivered fresh basil leaves
1 tablespoon vegetable oil
1 cup chopped yellow onion
2 teaspoons minced garlic
2 cups cooked long-grain white rice
½ cup minced fresh parsley
1½ teaspoons dried marjoram
¼ teaspoon salt
⅛ teaspoon red pepper flakes
1 cup (4 ounces) shredded ALPINE LACE® Reduced Fat Swiss Cheese

1. To parboil the peppers: Half-fill a large saucepan with cold water and bring to a boil over high heat. Using a small pointed knife, trim the top ½ inch off of the peppers and remove the seeds and ribs. To enable the peppers to stand up straight, trim about ¼ inch off of the bottoms, being careful not to cut through the bottoms. Simmer the peppers in the water, uncovered, for 2 to 3 minutes, then remove with tongs or a slotted spoon and drain.

2. To make the sauce: In a medium-size saucepan, bring the tomatoes, water and basil to a boil over medium-high heat. Set aside.

3. Preheat the oven to 350°F. Spray an 8-inch round baking dish with nonstick cooking spray.

4. To make the stuffing: In a small nonstick skillet, heat the oil over medium-high heat. Add the onion and garlic and sauté for 5 minutes or until soft. Remove the skillet from the heat. Stir in the rice, half of the tomato sauce, the parsley, marjoram, salt, red pepper flakes and cheese.

5. Stuff the rice mixture into the peppers, then stand them upright in the baking dish. Bake, uncovered, for 30 minutes. Top the peppers with the remaining tomato sauce and continue baking 10 minutes more or until the peppers are tender and the sauce is bubbly. Serve hot!   *Makes 6 servings*

Harvest Casserole

- 2 cups lentils, rinsed and cooked
- 2 cups fresh or frozen broccoli, chopped
- 1½ cups cooked rice
- 1¼ cups (5 ounces) shredded Cheddar cheese
- 1 tablespoon soy sauce
- ½ teaspoon salt (optional)
- ¼ teaspoon dried thyme leaves
- ¼ teaspoon dried marjoram leaves
- ¼ teaspoon dried rosemary
- 4 eggs
- 1 cup milk

Preheat oven to 350°F.

Combine lentils, broccoli, rice, cheese, soy sauce, salt, thyme, marjoram and rosemary in large bowl; mix well. Place mixture in greased 9-inch casserole dish.

Stir together eggs and milk in medium bowl. Pour egg mixture over lentil mixture. Bake 45 minutes or until lightly browned. Top with additional shredded Cheddar cheese, if desired. *Makes 8 servings*

Favorite recipe from **USA Dry Pea & Lentil Council**

Old Mexico Black Beans & Rice

- 2   **tablespoons vegetable oil**
- 1   **package (6.8 ounces) RICE-A-RONI®
      Spanish Rice**
- ½   **cup chopped green bell pepper**
- ½   **cup chopped onion**
- 2   **cloves garlic, minced**
- 1   **can (14½ ounces) tomatoes, undrained,
      chopped**
- ¼   **to ½ teaspoon hot pepper sauce**
- 1   **can (16 ounces) black beans, rinsed
      and drained**
- 1   **can (16 ounces) pinto beans, rinsed
      and drained**
- ½   **cup (2 ounces) shredded Cheddar
      cheese or Monterey Jack cheese**
- 2   **tablespoons chopped parsley or cilantro
      (optional)**

1. In large skillet, heat oil over medium heat. Add rice-vermicelli mix, green pepper, onion and garlic; sauté, stirring frequently, until vermicelli is golden brown.

2. Stir in 2 cups water, tomatoes, hot pepper sauce and contents of seasoning packet; bring to a boil over high heat.

3. Cover; reduce heat. Simmer 15 minutes.

4. Stir in black and pinto beans.

5. Cover; continue to simmer 5 minutes or until liquid is absorbed and rice is tender. Serve topped with cheese; sprinkle with parsley, if desired.

Makes 4 servings

Microwave Black Bean & Cream Cheese Enchiladas

1 cup frozen corn
⅔ cup chopped green bell pepper
½ cup chopped onion
1 package (8 ounces) low-fat cream
cheese
1 cup GUILTLESS GOURMET® Salsa
(mild, medium or hot), divided
10 corn tortillas (6 inches each)
10 tablespoons GUILTLESS GOURMET®
Black Bean Dip (mild or spicy)
1 cup GUILTLESS GOURMET® Nacho
Dip (mild or spicy)

Microwave Directions: Place corn, pepper and onion in 2-cup glass measure. Cover with vented plastic wrap; microwave on HIGH (100% power) 3 minutes or until heated through. Stir; let stand, covered, until ready to use. Cut cream cheese into 10 equal portions; roll each portion into long tube. Pour half the salsa in 13×9-inch glass baking dish.

To soften tortillas, stack 5 tortillas and wrap in damp paper towel; microwave on HIGH 35 seconds.

To assemble enchiladas, spread 1 tablespoon bean dip in center of each tortilla. Place 1 cheese tube on top of dip in center. Drizzle 1 heaping tablespoonful corn mixture over cheese. Roll up tortilla and place seam side down in dish. Repeat with remaining softened tortillas. Soften remaining 5 tortillas and assemble as

directed. Pour remaining ½ cup salsa over top. Pour
nacho dip over salsa. Cover with vented plastic wrap;
microwave on HIGH 10 minutes. Let stand 3 minutes
before serving.   *Makes 10 servings*

Pinto Bean & Zucchini Burritos

- 6 flour tortillas (6 inches each)
- ¾ cup GUILTLESS GOURMET® Pinto
  Bean Dip (mild or spicy)
- 2 teaspoons water
- 1 teaspoon olive oil
- 1 medium zucchini, chopped
- ¼ cup chopped green onions
- ¼ cup GUILTLESS GOURMET® Green
  Tomatillo Salsa
- 1 cup GUILTLESS GOURMET® Salsa
  (mild, medium or hot), divided
- 1½ cups shredded lettuce

Preheat oven to 300°F. Wrap tortillas in foil. Bake
10 minutes or until softened and heated through.
Meanwhile, combine bean dip and water in small bowl.
Heat oil in large skillet over medium-high heat until
hot. Add zucchini and onions. Cook and stir until
zucchini is crisp-tender; stir in bean dip mixture and
tomatillo salsa.

Fill each tortilla with zucchini mixture, dividing
evenly. Roll up tortillas; place on 6 individual serving
plates. Top with salsa. Serve hot with lettuce.

                                        Makes 6 servings

Chilaquiles

1 medium onion, chopped
2 tablespoons vegetable oil
1 can (28 ounces) whole tomatoes, cut up
1 package (1.25 ounces) LAWRY'S® Taco
   Spices & Seasonings
1 can (4 ounces) diced green chiles
   (optional)
6 ounces tortilla chips
4 cups (16 ounces) grated Monterey Jack
   cheese
1 cup dairy sour cream
½ cup (2 ounces) grated Cheddar cheese

In large skillet, sauté onion in oil. Add tomatoes, Taco
Spices & Seasonings and chiles; blend well. Simmer,
uncovered, 10 to 15 minutes. In lightly greased 2-quart
casserole, layer ½ each of tortilla chips, sauce and
Monterey Jack cheese. Repeat layers; top with sour
cream. Bake in 350°F oven 30 minutes. Sprinkle with
Cheddar cheese and bake 10 minutes longer. Let stand
15 minutes before cutting into squares.

Microwave Directions: In 2-quart microwave-safe bowl,
combine onion and oil; microwave on HIGH (100%
power) 2 to 2½ minutes until tender. Add tomatoes,
Taco Spices & Seasonings and green chiles; blend well.
Cover with waxed paper and microwave on HIGH
(100% power) 5 to 7 minutes. In 2-quart microwave-
safe casserole, layer ½ each of tortilla chips, sauce and
Monterey Jack cheese. Repeat layers. Cover with waxed

paper and microwave on HIGH (100% power) 12
minutes, rotating after 6 minutes. Top with sour cream
and sprinkle with Cheddar cheese. Microwave,
uncovered, on HIGH 2 minutes or until cheese is
melted. Let stand 3 minutes before cutting into
squares.   *Makes 6 to 8 servings*

Pasta Fagiole

1 **cup chopped onions**
2 **teaspoons minced garlic**
1 **tablespoon vegetable oil**
2 **(13¾-ounce) cans COLLEGE INN®**
   Chicken Broth
1 **(16-ounce) can stewed tomatoes**
½ **teaspoon dried basil leaves**
¼ **teaspoon red pepper flakes**
1 **(10-ounce) package frozen chopped**
   spinach, thawed and drained
1 **cup chick-peas, drained**
1 **cup cooked ditalini pasta**
   Grated Parmesan cheese

In 4-quart pot, over medium-high heat, sauté onions
and garlic in oil for 2 to 3 minutes or until tender.
Stir in broth, tomatoes, basil and red pepper flakes.
Heat to a boil; reduce heat. Simmer for 5 minutes.
Add spinach, chick-peas and pasta; simmer for 6 to
8 minutes or until heated through. Serve hot with
Parmesan cheese.   *Makes 8 servings*

Jamaican Black Bean Stew

2 cups brown rice
2 pounds sweet potatoes
3 pounds butternut squash
1 large onion, coarsely chopped
1 can (about 14 ounces) vegetable broth
3 cloves garlic, minced
1 tablespoon curry powder
1½ teaspoons allspice
½ teaspoon ground red pepper
¼ teaspoon salt
2 cans (15 ounces each) black beans,
    drained and rinsed
½ cup raisins
3 tablespoons fresh lime juice
1 cup diced tomato
1 cup diced, peeled cucumber

1. Prepare rice according to package directions. Peel sweet potatoes; cut into ¾-inch chunks to measure 4 cups. Peel squash; remove seeds. Cut flesh into ¾-inch cubes to measure 5 cups.

2. Combine potatoes, squash, onion, broth, garlic, curry powder, allspice, pepper and salt in Dutch oven. Bring to a boil; reduce heat to low. Simmer, covered, 5 minutes. Add beans and raisins. Simmer 5 minutes or just until sweet potatoes and squash are tender and beans are hot. Remove from heat; stir in lime juice.

3. Serve stew over brown rice; top with tomato and cucumber. *Makes 8 servings*

Spicy Tomato Chili with Red Beans

1 tablespoon olive oil
1 cup chopped onion
1 cup chopped green bell pepper
1 cup sliced celery
1 clove garlic, minced
1 can (15 ounces) diced tomatoes,
    undrained
1 can (15 ounces) red beans, rinsed and
    drained
1 can (10 ounces) diced tomatoes with
    green chilies
1 can (8 ounces) low-sodium tomato
    sauce
8 (6-inch) corn tortillas

1. Preheat oven to 400°F.

2. Heat oil in large saucepan over medium heat until hot. Add onion, bell pepper, celery and garlic. Cook and stir 5 minutes or until onion is translucent.

3. Add remaining ingredients except tortillas. Bring to a boil; reduce heat to low. Simmer, uncovered, 15 minutes.

4. Cut each tortilla into 8 wedges. Place on baking sheet; bake 8 minutes or until crisp. Crush about half of tortilla wedges; place in bottom of soup bowls. Spoon chili over tortillas. Serve with remaining tortilla wedges. *Makes 4 servings*

Hearty Vegetable Gumbo

Nonstick cooking spray
½ cup chopped onion
½ cup chopped green bell pepper
¼ cup chopped celery
2 cloves garlic, minced
2 cans (about 14 ounces each) stewed
   tomatoes, undrained
2 cups no-salt-added tomato juice
1 can (15 ounces) red beans, rinsed and
   drained
1 tablespoon chopped fresh parsley
¼ teaspoon dried oregano leaves
¼ teaspoon hot pepper sauce
2 bay leaves
1½ cups quick-cooking brown rice
1 package (10 ounces) frozen chopped
   okra, thawed

1. Spray 4-quart Dutch oven with cooking spray; heat over medium heat until hot. Add onion, bell pepper, celery and garlic. Cook and stir 3 minutes or until crisp-tender.

2. Add stewed tomatoes, juice, beans, parsley, oregano, pepper sauce and bay leaves. Bring to a boil over high heat. Add rice. Reduce heat to medium-low. Simmer, covered, 15 minutes or until rice is tender.

3. Add okra; simmer, covered, 5 minutes more or until okra is tender. Remove bay leaves; discard.

Makes 4 (2-cup) servings

Tuscan Vegetable Stew

2 tablespoons olive oil
2 teaspoons bottled minced garlic
2 packages (4 ounces each) sliced mixed
     exotic mushrooms *or* 1 package
     (8 ounces) sliced button mushrooms
¼ cup sliced shallots
1 jar (7 ounces) roasted red peppers
1 can (14½ ounces) Italian-style stewed
     tomatoes, undrained
1 can (19 ounces) cannellini beans,
     drained
1 bunch fresh basil
1 tablespoon balsamic vinegar
   Grated Romano, Parmesan or Asiago
     cheese

1. Heat oil and garlic in large deep skillet over medium
heat. Add mushrooms and shallots; cook 5 minutes,
stirring occasionally.

2. While mushroom mixture is cooking, drain and
rinse peppers; cut into 1-inch pieces. Drain tomatoes,
reserving juice. Coarsely chop tomatoes.

3. Add peppers, tomatoes and beans to skillet; bring to
a boil. Reduce heat to medium-low. Cover and simmer
10 minutes, stirring once.

4. While stew is simmering, cut basil leaves into thin
strips to measure ¼ cup packed. Stir basil and vinegar
into stew; add salt and pepper to taste. Sprinkle with
cheese.   *Makes 4 servings*

Minestrone alla Milanese

¼ pound green beans
2 medium zucchini
1 large potato
½ pound cabbage
⅓ cup olive oil
3 tablespoons butter or margarine
2 medium onions, chopped
3 medium carrots, coarsely chopped
3 ribs celery, coarsely chopped
1 clove garlic, minced
1 can (28 ounces) Italian plum tomatoes, undrained
3½ cups beef broth
1½ cups water
½ teaspoon salt
½ teaspoon dried basil leaves
¼ teaspoon dried rosemary
¼ teaspoon pepper
1 bay leaf
1 can (16 ounces) cannellini beans
Freshly grated Parmesan cheese (optional)

1. Trim green beans; cut into 1-inch pieces. Trim zucchini; cut into ½-inch cubes. Peel potato; cut into ¾-inch cubes. Coarsely shred cabbage.

2. Heat oil and butter in 6-quart stockpot or Dutch oven over medium heat. Add onions; cook and stir 6 to 8 minutes until onions are soft and golden but not brown. Stir in carrots and potato; cook and stir 5 minutes. Stir in celery and green beans; cook and stir 5 minutes. Stir in zucchini; cook and stir 3 minutes. Stir in cabbage and garlic; cook and stir 1 minute more.

3. Drain tomatoes, reserving juice. Add broth, water and reserved juice to stockpot. Chop tomatoes coarsely; add to stockpot. Stir in salt, basil, rosemary, pepper and bay leaf. Bring to a boil over high heat; reduce heat to low. Cover and simmer 1½ hours, stirring occasionally.

4. Rinse and drain cannellini beans; add beans to stockpot. Uncover and cook over medium-low heat 30 to 40 minutes more until soup thickens, stirring occasionally. Remove bay leaf. Serve with cheese.

Makes 8 to 10 servings (about 12 cups)

Sesame Peanut Spaghetti Squash

Nonstick cooking spray
1 spaghetti squash (about 3 pounds)
⅓ cup sesame seeds
⅓ cup vegetable broth
2 tablespoons reduced-sodium soy sauce
1 tablespoon sugar
2 teaspoons sesame oil
1 teaspoon cornstarch
1 teaspoon crushed red pepper
1 teaspoon Worcestershire sauce
1 tablespoon vegetable oil
2 medium carrots, julienned
1 large red bell pepper, seeded and thinly sliced
¼ pound fresh snow peas (Chinese pea pods), cut diagonally in half
½ cup coarsely chopped unsalted peanuts
⅓ cup minced fresh cilantro

1. Preheat oven to 350°F. Spray 13×9-inch baking dish with cooking spray. Wash squash; cut in half lengthwise. Remove and discard seeds. Place squash, cut-side down, in prepared dish. Bake 45 minutes to 1 hour or until just tender.

2. Using fork and oven mitts to protect hands, remove spaghetti-like strands from hot squash; place in large bowl. Cover and keep warm.

3. Heat wok over medium-high heat until hot. Add sesame seeds; cook and stir 45 seconds or until golden brown. Remove to blender. Add broth, soy sauce, sugar, sesame oil, cornstarch, crushed red pepper and Worcestershire sauce. Process until mixture is puréed.

4. Heat wok or large skillet over medium-high heat 1 minute or until hot. Drizzle vegetable oil into wok; heat 30 seconds. Add carrots; stir-fry 1 minute. Add bell pepper; stir-fry 2 minutes or until vegetables are crisp-tender. Add snow peas; stir-fry 1 minute. Stir sesame seed mixture; add to wok. Cook and stir 1 minute or until sauce is thickened.

5. Pour vegetable mixture over spaghetti squash. Add peanuts and cilantro; toss well.   *Makes 4 servings*

Vegetable Stir-Fry in Spicy Black Bean Sauce

1   teaspoon vegetable oil
1   medium onion, chopped
1   medium-size green bell pepper, cut into
        strips
3   carrots, cut into julienne strips
        (matchstick size)
3   cups shredded cabbage (green, red or
        napa)
1   cup tofu, crumbled
4   cups cooked rice, kept warm

BLACK BEAN SAUCE
1   cup GUILTLESS GOURMET® Spicy
        Black Bean Dip
2   teaspoons water
¼   cup low-sodium soy sauce
¼   cup cooking sherry
1   tablespoon minced peeled ginger root
1   clove garlic, minced

Heat oil in wok or large skillet over medium-high heat until hot. Add onion, pepper, carrots, cabbage and tofu; stir-fry until crisp-tender.

To prepare Black Bean Sauce, combine bean dip and water in small bowl; mix well. Stir in remaining Black Bean Sauce ingredients; pour over stir-fried vegetables. Stir-fry over high heat 2 minutes more. Reduce heat to low; cook 2 to 4 minutes more or until heated through, stirring often. Serve over hot rice.

Makes 6 servings

Zesty Mixed Vegetables

2 green onions with tops
1 or 2 jalapeño or Thai chili peppers*
2 tablespoons vegetable oil
8 ounces green beans, trimmed and sliced
   diagonally into thirds
2 cups cauliflower florets
2 cloves garlic, chopped
8 ounces peeled fresh baby carrots
1 cup chicken broth, divided
1 tablespoon cornstarch
1 teaspoon sugar
¼ teaspoon salt
2 tablespoons oyster sauce

• Cut onions into ½-inch pieces; keep white part and green tops of onions in separate piles. Cut jalapeño lengthwise in half. Remove stem and seeds. Cut jalapeño crosswise into thin slices.

• Heat wok over high heat about 1 minute or until hot. Drizzle oil into wok and heat 30 seconds. Add white part of onions, jalapeño, beans, cauliflower and garlic; stir-fry until tender. Add carrots and ¾ cup broth. Cover; bring to a boil. Reduce heat to low; cook until carrots and beans are crisp-tender.

• Combine cornstarch, sugar and salt in cup; stir in remaining ¼ cup broth and oyster sauce until smooth. Stir into wok. Cook until sauce boils and thickens. Stir in onion tops.   *Makes 4 servings*

*Jalapeños can sting and irritate the skin; wear rubber gloves when handling jalapeños and do not touch eyes. Wash hands after handling.

Roasted Vegetables with Noodles

5   tablespoons soy sauce, divided
3   tablespoons peanut or vegetable oil
2   tablespoons rice vinegar
2   cloves garlic, minced
1   teaspoon sugar
½   pound large fresh mushrooms
4   ounces shallots
1   medium zucchini squash, cut into
      1-inch pieces
1   medium yellow crookneck squash, cut
      into 1-inch pieces
1   red bell pepper, cut into 1-inch pieces
1   yellow bell pepper, cut into 1-inch
      pieces
2   small Oriental eggplants, cut into
      ½-inch slices *or* 2 cups cubed
      eggplant
8   ounces Chinese egg noodles or
      vermicelli, hot cooked and drained
1   tablespoon dark sesame oil

1. Preheat oven to 425°F. Combine 2 tablespoons soy sauce, peanut oil, vinegar, garlic and sugar in small bowl; mix well.

2. Combine vegetables in shallow roasting pan. (Do not line pan with foil.) Toss with soy sauce mixture to coat well.

3. Roast vegetables 20 minutes or until browned and tender, stirring well after 10 minutes.

4. Place noodles in large bowl. Toss hot noodles with remaining 3 tablespoons soy sauce and sesame oil.

5. Toss roasted vegetables with noodle mixture; serve warm or at room temperature.   *Makes 6 servings*

Pasta Primavera

     2   **tablespoons vegetable oil**
     ½   **cup sliced mushrooms**
     ¼   **cup sliced green onions**
     1   **clove garlic, minced**
     1   **cup cherry tomato halves**
     1   **can (15 ounces) VEG-ALL® Mixed Vegetables, drained**
     ½   **cup half-and-half**
     ½   **cup grated Parmesan cheese**
     2   **tablespoons chopped fresh basil leaves Salt and pepper to taste**
     4   **ounces uncooked spaghetti, cooked, drained**

1. Heat oil in large skillet. Add mushrooms, green onions and garlic; cook and stir 2 to 3 minutes.

2. Add tomato halves; cook 1 minute, stirring gently. Set aside.

3. Combine VEG-ALL®, half-and-half, cheese and basil in medium saucepan; cook over medium heat until just heated through. Season with salt and pepper. Stir in hot pasta and tomato mixture; serve immediately.

Makes 4 servings

Soba Stir-Fry

8 ounces uncooked soba noodles
  (Japanese buckwheat pasta)
1 tablespoon light olive oil
2 cups sliced fresh shiitake mushrooms
1 medium red bell pepper, cut into thin
  strips
2 whole dried red peppers *or* ¼ teaspoon
  crushed red pepper
1 clove garlic, minced
2 cups shredded napa cabbage
½ cup reduced-sodium chicken broth
2 tablespoons reduced-sodium tamari or
  soy sauce
1 tablespoon rice wine or dry sherry
2 teaspoons cornstarch
1 package (14 ounces) firm tofu, drained
  and cut into 1-inch cubes
2 green onions, thinly sliced

1. Cook noodles according to package directions, omitting salt. Drain and set aside.

2. Heat oil in large nonstick skillet or wok over medium heat. Add mushrooms, bell pepper, dried peppers and garlic. Cook 3 minutes or until mushrooms are tender.

3. Add cabbage. Cover. Cook 2 minutes or until cabbage is wilted.

4. Combine chicken broth, tamari, rice wine and cornstarch in small bowl. Stir sauce into vegetable mixture. Cook 2 minutes or until sauce is bubbly.

5. Stir in tofu and noodles; toss gently until heated through. Sprinkle with green onions. Serve immediately. *Makes 4 (2-cup) servings*

Tomato-Zucchini Pesto

 6 **ounces pasta**
 1 **cup fresh basil, chopped**
 1 **teaspoon vegetable oil**
 2 **cloves garlic, minced**
 1 **teaspoon sugar**
 ¼ **cup part-skim ricotta cheese**
 1 **tablespoon grated Parmesan cheese**
 1 **medium zucchini, cut into ¼-inch-thick slices**
 2 **teaspoons water**
 1 **cup cherry tomatoes, quartered**
 ½ **teaspoon salt (optional)**

Prepare pasta as directed on package; rinse and drain. Cover and set aside. In food processor or blender, process basil, oil, garlic and sugar. Blend in cheeses; set aside. Place zucchini in large casserole dish. Add water; cover. Microwave on HIGH 4 minutes; drain. Stir in pasta and Parmesan cheese mixture. Garnish with tomatoes. Season with salt, if desired.

Makes 4 servings

Favorite recipe from **The Sugar Association, Inc.**

Vegetable Risotto

2 tablespoons olive oil, divided
1 medium zucchini, cubed
1 medium yellow summer squash, cubed
1 cup shiitake mushroom slices
1 cup chopped onions
1 clove garlic, minced
6 plum tomatoes, quartered and seeded
1 teaspoon dried oregano leaves
3 cups vegetable stock
¾ cup uncooked arborio rice
¼ cup grated Parmesan cheese
    Salt and pepper
½ cup frozen peas, thawed

1. Heat 1 tablespoon oil in large saucepan over medium heat until hot. Add zucchini and summer squash; cook and stir 5 minutes or until crisp-tender. Place in medium bowl; set aside.

2. Add mushrooms, onions and garlic to saucepan; cook and stir 5 minutes or until tender. Add tomatoes and oregano; cook and stir 2 to 3 minutes or until tomatoes are soft. Place in bowl with zucchini mixture. Wipe saucepan clean with paper towels.

3. Place stock in small saucepan; bring to a boil over medium heat. Reduce heat to medium-low to keep stock hot, but not boiling.

4. Meanwhile, heat remaining 1 tablespoon oil in saucepan over medium heat until hot. Add rice; cook and stir 2 minutes.

5. Add ¾ cup stock to rice. Reduce heat to medium-low, maintaining a simmer throughout addition of stock and cooking of rice. Cook and stir until rice has absorbed stock. Repeat, adding stock 3 more times, cooking and stirring until rice has absorbed stock. (Total cooking time of rice will be about 20 to 25 minutes.)

6. Stir cheese into rice mixture. Season to taste with salt and pepper. Stir in reserved vegetables and peas; cook until heated through.   *Makes 4 to 6 servings*

Indian Vegetable Curry

2 **to 3 teaspoons curry powder**
1 **can (16 ounces) sliced potatoes,**
    drained
1 **bag (16 ounces) BIRDS EYE® frozen**
    Farm Fresh Mixtures Broccoli,
    Cauliflower and Carrots
1 **can (15 ounces) chick-peas, drained**
1 **can (14½ ounces) stewed tomatoes**
1 **can (13¾ ounces) vegetable or chicken**
    broth
2 **tablespoons cornstarch**

• Stir curry powder in large skillet over high heat until fragrant, about 30 seconds.

• Stir in potatoes, vegetables, chick-peas and tomatoes; bring to boil. Reduce heat to medium-high; cover and cook 8 minutes.

• Blend broth with cornstarch; stir into vegetables. Cook until thickened.   *Makes about 6 servings*

Red Beans and Rice

Nonstick cooking spray
1 cup chopped onion
½ cup chopped celery
½ cup chopped green bell pepper
3 cloves garlic, minced
2 cans (15 ounces each) red beans,
   rinsed and drained
1 can (8 ounces) tomato sauce
1 teaspoon Worcestershire sauce
1 teaspoon Cajun or Creole seasoning
¼ teaspoon ground red pepper
¼ teaspoon hot pepper sauce
3 cups hot cooked rice
   Additional hot pepper sauce (optional)

Spray Dutch oven with nonstick cooking spray and
heat over medium-high heat until hot. Add onion,
celery, bell pepper and garlic. Cook and stir 2 to 3
minutes. Add beans, tomato sauce, Worcestershire
sauce, Cajun seasonings, red pepper and pepper sauce.
Reduce heat; cover and simmer 15 minutes. Serve
beans with rice and additional pepper sauce, if desired.

Makes 6 servings

The publishers would like to thank the companies and organizations listed below for the use of their recipes and photographs in this publication.

Alpine Lace Brands, Inc.
American Lamb Council
Birds Eye
Blue Diamond Growers
Bob Evans Farms®
Dean Foods Vegetable Company
Del Monte Corporation
Dole Food Company, Inc.
Filippo Berio Olive Oil
Florida Department of Agriculture and Consumer Services, Bureau of Seafood and Aquaculture
Golden Grain/Mission Pasta
Guiltless Gourmet, Incorporated
Hormel Foods Corporation
The HVR Company
Kraft Foods, Inc.
Lawry's® Foods, Inc.
Minnesota Cultivated Wild Rice Council
MOTT'S® Inc., a division of Cadbury Beverages Inc.

Nabisco, Inc.
National Foods, Inc.
National Honey Board
National Turkey Federation
Nestlé Food Company
North Dakota Wheat Commission
Perdue Farms Incorporated
The Procter & Gamble Company
RED STAR® Yeast & Products, A Division of Universal Foods Corporation
Reckitt & Colman Inc.
Sargento® Foods Inc.
Southeast United Dairy Industry Association, Inc.
StarKist® Seafood Company
The Sugar Association
USA Dry Pea & Lentil Council
USA Rice Council
Walnut Marketing Board
Wisconsin Milk Marketing Board

VOLUME MEASUREMENTS (dry)

1/8 teaspoon = 0.5 mL
1/4 teaspoon = 1 mL
1/2 teaspoon = 2 mL
3/4 teaspoon = 4 mL
1 teaspoon = 5 mL
1 tablespoon = 15 mL
2 tablespoons = 30 mL
1/4 cup = 60 mL
1/3 cup = 75 mL
1/2 cup = 125 mL
2/3 cup = 150 mL
3/4 cup = 175 mL
1 cup = 250 mL
2 cups = 1 pint = 500 mL
3 cups = 750 mL
4 cups = 1 quart = 1 L

VOLUME MEASUREMENTS (fluid)

1 fluid ounce (2 tablespoons) = 30 mL
4 fluid ounces (1/2 cup) = 125 mL
8 fluid ounces (1 cup) = 250 mL
12 fluid ounces (1 1/2 cups) = 375 mL
16 fluid ounces (2 cups) = 500 mL

WEIGHTS (mass)

1/2 ounce = 15 g
1 ounce = 30 g
3 ounces = 90 g
4 ounces = 120 g
8 ounces = 225 g
10 ounces = 285 g
12 ounces = 360 g
16 ounces = 1 pound = 450 g

DIMENSIONS

1/16 inch = 2 mm
1/8 inch = 3 mm
1/4 inch = 6 mm
1/2 inch = 1.5 cm
3/4 inch = 2 cm
1 inch = 2.5 cm

OVEN TEMPERATURES

250°F = 120°C
275°F = 140°C
300°F = 150°C
325°F = 160°C
350°F = 180°C
375°F = 190°C
400°F = 200°C
425°F = 220°C
450°F = 230°C

BAKING PAN SIZES

Utensil	Size in Inches/ Quarts	Metric Volume	Size in Centimeters
Baking or Cake Pan (square or rectangular)	8×8×2	2 L	20×20×5
	9×9×2	2.5 L	23×23×5
	12×8×2	3 L	30×20×5
	13×9×2	3.5 L	33×23×5
Loaf Pan	8×4×3	1.5 L	20×10×7
	9×5×3	2 L	23×13×7
Round Layer Cake Pan	8×1½	1.2 L	20×4
	9×1½	1.5 L	23×4
Pie Plate	8×1¼	750 mL	20×3
	9×1¼	1 L	23×3
Baking Dish or Casserole	1 quart	1 L	—
	1½ quart	1.5 L	—
	2 quart	2 L	—